THE SYSTEM

A SYSTEMATIC YIELD SYSTEM TO ENSLAVE MAN KIND

The New World Order Waiting in the Wings

Brandon P. Holcombe

Before I begin this book, I would first like to give honor and thanks to God, the Creator of all things. I dedicate this book in His honor because it is He who's given us everything that we know and don't know. I pray for wisdom, guidance, and courage to interpret the things that I see, hear, and feel. It is He who has implanted me with the wisdom to deliver the truth to the people when they so desperately need it. Today we live in a society that has clouded our true essence as human beings and that is to serve, glorify, and obey God.

By not doing the things that He has asked of us we have subjected ourselves to the horrors of the world. By writing this book I may be putting myself and my family in jeopardy. For this reason alone it may result in unwanted attention to me and my family. There are things that you will not understand or not believe until they have come to past. It is my sincere hope that whoever reads this will be enlightened and strengthened to the point of no return. Also, to the ones that are still skeptical about the contents and reasons for this book, I pray for your souls.

To give you a better understanding of the book I first need to give you insight on who I am and what has driven me to take action. I was born in the early '70s when the war in Vietnam was prevalent and the desire to bring our troops home was followed by the desire for peace. I was raised on a farm; the land was given to my mother by her mother. I grew up in a very small town with what many would consider is a large family – five sisters and three brothers.

My parents didn't make a lot of money, but we always had the things we needed and not the things we wanted. This is something that I will touch on more in chapters to come because it is one of the underlying reasons for the state of things in our country and the world. As I grew up in a large household, there was always structure and guidance. My mother was consistently in church so I can say that I grew up in a Christian-based family. So my views and ideas of life and religion were guided at a very young age.

In my adolescent years, I was very quiet and shy, but not in my household. In my household there was always competition, but I believe it was in a good way. When I was young and anyone spoke about Revelation or things happening in the world that pertained to the Bible, I would get so scared I would have to leave the conversation. Whenever I heard anyone speak about the Book of Revelation I would get scared. There are many reasons why I felt this fear, but the main one I acknowledge is that it was what I didn't want to happen.

Fear is one of the things that causes people to not act because in the system people get comfortable in their lifestyles. From the day you are born you are taught that the system is comfortable and safe and will provide you with everything you need. But the system is actually the opposite of that because it provides you with the things you want and not necessarily the things you need. When you are raised in the system you become comfortable within your lifestyle and the way you live so that you only see that and nothing else. So it took me a long time to see things for what they are and most of it came to me when I graduated from High School and enlisted into the Armed Forces.

As I was growing up I was very sheltered, but once I left home I began to see what the world was really like. Experiencing different races, beliefs, and cultures gave me insight and shaped me to be the person I am today. So before I explain to you what the SYSTEM is, I would like to applaud the people in the U.S. and around the world who have stood up and want to be heard on their issues. That is the main reason why I am writing today, so that I can explain to them that they are headed in the right direction but doing it in the wrong way. Occupy Wall Street, and all the other occupy movements are great but when you ask someone who is involved what they are protesting about (which I did) they will say many things.

Like to "stop corruption," or "create jobs," or "for better health care." One person told me "for less government control." That is fine and all these complaints have merit but doing these things (protesting in this manner) will actually create more control. By the time I have finished this book many people will have grown tired of the way things are and it will eventually only end in violence. This has already happened in one state; violence erupted and one person got killed.

So my question to the protesters of the occupy movements and anyone else who is fed up with the way things are is this: What did you do to cause or help create the situation we are in today? The situation I am referring to is control. If you don't know it, the System, as I call it, has control of every aspect of my and your life. It may sound crazy but it is the truth beyond belief. What if I told you that the System has been in place for hundreds of years and we as people have been puppets in the biggest most elaborate and most controlled chess game in the history of mankind? From the time you were been born to now you will be a part of the System.

In the chapters ahead I will explain in detail what the System is, who created it, and for what purpose it was created. I will also discuss the timeline from the start to now and explain how you can separate yourself from it. So this is not a doomsday book, but a book about faith and hope that things can change. The only way it can change is to look within ourselves. So when you begin this book start with an open mind and heart and you will be enlightened with the knowledge and wisdom to change.

The System

The Systematic Yielded System to Enslave Mankind

New World Order Waiting in the Wings

1. What is the System, When Was It Created, and By Whom?
A. God and the Creation of the Heavens
B. Angels and the War in Heaven: The First Rebellion
C. Demons and the Rise and Fall of Mankind
D. Enoch and Daughter of Mankind: The Second Rebellion (The Watchers)
E. The Rise of Nephilim (The Flood of Noah) and Fall of The???

2. Did the Knowledge of the Fallen Angels Perish with Them?
A. Ancient Egypt and the Pyramids: Their True Purpose
B. The Maya Civilization and the Continuance of Demonic Rituals
C. Government: The Creation of Democracy and Communism
D. Can a Democracy Lead To Communism?
E. The Roman Empire and Jesus Christ
F. Roman Catholic Church and Its Pursuit to Destroy Radical Views

3.   The Rise of Secret Societies Which May Be Demonic in Nature

Chapter 1

What Is The System, When Was It Created, And By Whom?

GOD AND THE CREATION OF THE HEAVENS

Since the beginning of our conception we have been a part of a system which has been working to control every aspect of our lives. In the chapters ahead I will discuss when and who created the system and what is the overall objective. In order to give a complete conception of the system I would like to start with the beginning of time and with God. So what or who is God? In English God is the given name for a single being in deistic and theistic religions (and other belief systems) who is either the sole deity in monotheism, or a single deity in polytheism.

The overseer and supernatural creator of the universe is how God is perceived. There are a variety of attributes that Theologians have given to God. Omni benevolence (perfect goodness), omniscience (infinite knowledge), omnipresence (present everywhere), omnipotence (infinite power), and eternal are some of the most common, but necessary attributes.

ANGELS AND THE WAR IN HEAVEN:

THE FIRST REBELLION

God is the creator of all things, the beginning
and the end as in Revelation Chapter 1 verse 8.
"I am Alpha and Omega, the beginning and the
ending, said the Lord, which is, and which was,
and which is to come, the Almighty." In his divine
love and wisdom he created the entire universe.
Also in his divine wisdom and knowledge he created
Angels. In Greek the word Angel or "Angelo's"
means "messenger."

Angels are seen as attendants or agents of God or
messenger in Jewish, Muslim, and Christian
theologies. The will of God is usually carried out
or imparted by Angels as seen in the Bible.
Sometime after the creation of Angels, through
God's divine love and wisdom, He created man.
There is a general belief that at some point in
time Lucifer joined forces with a third of the
Angels in heaven in an attempt to overthrow God
and his faithful Angels. A popular theory about
the cause of the conflict is that when God created
man he asked all of his Angels to bow before his
new creation.

At the time Lucifer was one of the highest
Archangels and thought this was too humbling so he
refused to degrade himself in this way and then
asked "a son of fire should be forced to bow
before a son of clay." A theory that is very
similar is one that suggests that Lucifer should
bow to Jesus. It seems that Lucifer was

outgrowing the post as the highest of chief angels
and the Seraphim. So how many Angels were
involved in the war in Heaven? According to
Bishop of Tusculum in the 15th century it was
estimated that 133,306,668 Angles fell from the
Heavens in a total of nine days and this was
reaffirmed by Alphorns. De Spina (c.1460).

When the war actually took place is another
question to think about because there is no
mention in Hebraic writings or the Old Testament
about the Fallen Angels or Hell. The time for the
battle to occur possibly lies somewhere between
the Old and New Testament because of the part that
Satan plays in the Bible. Christ made it clear
that Satan/Lucifer is the enemy. In the book of
Revelation Satan appears as a dragon with ten
heads and does battle with the Armies of God, lead
my Michael the Archangel. Another belief is that
the war continued for many days with Lucifer and
his followers building war machines and gaining a
superior position over Michael and the Angels. The
final result is that Michael and the Angels
crushed Satan and his followers.

Revelation 12:7-10 Michael the Archangel defeats
the Great Dragon. A supernatural battle occurs
between the Angels of God and the Fallen Angels of
Satan.

7. And there was war in heaven Michael and his
Angels fought against the Dragon; and the Dragon
fought and his Angels

8. And world, he was cast out into the earth, and
his Angels were cast out with him.

9. And the great Dragon was cast out, that Old
Serpent, call the Devil, and Satan, which deceived

the whole world, he was cast out into the Earth, and his Angels were cast out with him.

10. And I heard a loud voice saying in Heaven "Now is come Salvation, and strength, and the Kingdom of our God, and the Power of his Christ; for the Accuser of our Brethren is cast down which accused them before our God Day and Night.

Now let's go back to the creation of man in the book of Genesis 1:26 through 3:24

1:26 And God said, Let us make man in our image, after our likeness: and let them have dominion over the fish of the sea, and over the fowl of the air, and over the cattle, and over all the earth, and over every creeping thing that crept upon the earth.

1:27 So God created man in his own image, in the image of God created he him; male and female created he them.

1:28 And God blessed them, and God said unto them, be fruitful, and multiply, and replenish the earth, and subdue it: and have dominion over the fish of the sea.

1:29 And God said, Behold, I have given you every herb bearing seed, which is upon the face of all the earth, and every tree, in the which is the fruit of a tree yielding seed; to you it shall be for meat.

1:30 And to every beast of the earth, and to every fowl of the air, and to everything that crept upon the earth, wherein there is life, I have given every green herb for meat: and it was so.

1:31 And God saw everything that he had made, and, behold, it was very good. And the evening and the morning were the sixth day.

2:1 Thus the heavens and the earth were finished and all the host of them.

2:2 And on the seventh day, God ended his work which he had made; and he rested on the seventh day from all his work which he had made.

2:3 And God blessed the seventh day, and sanctified it: because that in it he had rested from all his work which God created and made.

2:4 These are the generations of the heavens and of the earth when they were created, in the day that the LORD God made the earth and the heavens,

2:5 and every plant of the field before it was in the earth, and every herb of the field before it grew: for the Lord God had not caused it to rain upon the earth, and there was not a man to till the ground.

2:6 but there went up a mist

So can you say that Lucifer was a product of his environment or was he enacting his free will to act as he wished? Popular belief states that Angels don't have free will, but the rebellion in heaven would lead one to believe something quite different. Accounts from the Bible set the scene in heaven as joys, beautiful and majestic beyond our wildest dreams as seen in Revelation 21:10-27:10.

10. And he carried me away in the Spirit to a mountain great and high, and showed me the Holy City, Jerusalem, coming down out of heaven from God.

11. It shone with the glory of God, and its brilliance was like that of a very precious jewel, like jasper, clear as crystal.

12. It had a great, high wall with twelve gates and with twelve angels at the gates. On the gates were written the names of the twelve tribes of Israel.

13. There were three gates on the east, three on the north, three on the south and three on the west.

14. The wall of the city had twelve foundations, and on them were the names of the twelve apostles of the Lamb.

15. The angel who talked with me had a measuring rod of gold to measure the city, its gates and its walls.

16. The city was laid out like a square, as long as it was wide. He measured the city with the rod and found it to be 12,000 stadia [or 1,400 miles!] in length, and as wide and high as it is long [1,400 miles wide and tall!].

17. The angel measured the wall using human measurement, and it was 144 cubits [that is 200 feet!] thick.

18. The wall was made of jasper, and the city of pure gold, as pure as glass. The foundations of the city walls were decorated with every kind of precious stone. The first foundation was jasper,

the second sapphire, the third agate, the fourth emerald,

20. the fifth onyx, the sixth ruby, the seventh chrysolite, the eighth beryl, the ninth topaz, the tenth turquoise, the eleventh jacinth, and the twelfth amethyst [these last two stones are unknown or only exist in heaven today].

21. The twelve gates were twelve pearls, each gate made of a single pearl. The great street of the city was of gold, as pure as transparent glass.

22. I did not see a temple in the city, because the Lord God Almighty and the Lamb is its temple.

23. The city does not need the sun or the moon to shine on it, for the glory of God gives it light, and the Lamb is its lamp.

24. The nations will walk by its light, and the kings of the earth will bring their splendor into it.

25. On no day will its gates ever be shut, for there will be no night there.

26. The glory and honor of the nations will be brought into it.

27. Nothing impure will ever enter it, nor will anyone who does what is shameful or deceitful, but only those whose names are written in the Lamb's book of life.

This is one of the great descriptions in the Bible of heaven as revealed to John. Why would any Angel or human ever want to be removed from such a beautiful place? Lucifer and his followers foresaw a different ending but none-the-less they were kicked out of heaven by Michael and the rest of the Angels. When we think about heaven we think about a place. What if heaven was not a place nor a time but another dimension in which time and space does not exist?

Lucifer was casted out of heaven; he was cast to another dimension, which is our dimension and time. As accounted in the Bible he appears as a serpent to Eve. God punished the serpent by changing its form. It wasn't until after this punishment that the serpent became an animal that would grovel in the dust and crawl on its belly according to Genesis 3:14:

So the Lord God said to the serpent, "Because you have done this, you will be punished. You are singled out from all the domestic and wild animals of the whole earth to be cursed. You will grovel in the dust as long as live, crawling along your belly"

DEMONS AND THE RISE AND FALL OF MANKIND

It is under much speculation that Lucifer and his followers were on the earth after the creation of Adam and Eve and will be discussed a little later. Lucifer's followers were Angels, but once they fell from heaven or glory they became demonic in nature. What exactly are Demons? Demons are evil spirits that are opposed to God and his work. They appear to be fallen angels as referenced in the New Testament in 2 Peter 2:4 and Jude 6.

2 Peter 2:4 For if God did not spare angels when they sinned, but cast them into hell and committed them to pits of darkness, reserved for judgment…

Jude 6 And angels who did not keep their own domain, but abandoned their proper abode, He has kept in eternal bonds under darkness for the judgment of the great day.

The conclusion is that Lucifer and his followers began the SYSTEM when Lucifer tempted Eve to eat from the tree of knowledge of good and evil as seen in Genesis 3:1-24.

1. Now the serpent was more subtle than any other wild creature that the LORD God had made. He said to the woman, "Did God say, 'You shall not eat of any tree of the garden?'"

2. And the woman said to the serpent, "We may eat of the fruit of the trees of the garden,

3. but God said, 'You shall not eat of the fruit of the tree which is in the midst of the garden neither shall you touch it, lest you die.'"

4. But the serpent said to the woman, "You will not die.

5. For God knows that when you eat of it your eyes will be opened, and you will be like God, knowing good and evil."

6. So when the woman saw that the tree was good for food, and that it was a delight to the eyes, and that the tree was to be desired to make one wise, she took of its fruit and ate; and she also gave some to her husband, and he ate.

7. Then the eyes of both were opened, and they knew that they were naked; and they sewed fig leaves together and made themselves aprons.

8. And they heard the sound of the Lord God walking in the garden in the cool of the day, and the man and his wife hid themselves from the presence of the Lord God among the tree of the garden.

9. But the Lord God called to the man, and said to him "Where are you?"

10. And he said, "I heard the sound of thee in the garden, and I was afraid, because I was naked; and I hid myself."

11. He said, "Who told you that you were naked? Have you eaten from the tree of which I commanded you not to eat?"

12. The man said, "The woman whom thou gavest to be with me, she gave me fruit of the tree, and I ate."

13. Then the Lord God said to the woman, "What is this that you have done?" The woman said, "The serpent beguiled me, and I ate."

14. Then Lord God said to the serpent, "Because you have done this, cursed are you above all cattle, and above all wild animals; upon your belly you shall go, and dust you shall eat all the days of your life.

15. I will put enmity between you and the woman, and between your seed and her seed; he shall bruise your head, and you shall bruise his heel".

16. To the woman he said, "I will greatly multiply your pain in childbearing; in pain you shall bring forth children, yet your desire shall be for your husband, and he shall rule over you."

17. And to Adam he said, "Because you have listened to the voice of your wife, and have eaten of the tree of which I commanded you, you shall not eat of it, cursed is the ground because of you; in toil you shall eat of it all the days of your life;

18. thorns and thistles it shall bring forth to you; and you shall eat the plants of the field.

19. In the sweat of your face you shall eat bread till you return to the ground, for out of it you were taken; you are dust, and to dust you shall return."

20. The man called his wife name Eve, because she was the mother of all living.

21. And the LORD God made for Adam and for his wife garments to skins, and clothed them.

22. Then the LORD forth his hand and take also of the tree of life, and eat, and live forever"

23. Therefore the LORD God sent him forth from the Garden of Eden, to till the ground from which he was taken.

24. He drove out the man; and at the east of the Garden of Eden he placed the cherubim, and a flaming sword which turned every way, to guard the way to the tree of life.

ENOCH AND THE DAUGHTERS OF MANKIND:

THE SECOND REBELLION

Lucifer's objective was to take control of one of
God's most prized possessions, that is, Mankind.
Once Adam and Eve sinned and were cast out of the
Garden of Eden, they began to populate the earth.
And there were daughters of man on the earth.
This passage is referenced from one of the books
of Enoch. Extraordinary as this can be, there were
many prophets in the Bible, but Enoch, one of the
greatest prophets ever, is barely mentioned in the
Bible.

Well, who exactly is Enoch? As accounted from the
Bible he was the son of Jared Genesis 5:18-20,
which says, "When Jared had lived 162 years, he
became the father of Enoch." Genesis 5:21-24
continues, "When Enoch had lived 65 years, he
became the father of Methuselah. After he became
the father of Methuselah, Enoch walked faithfully
with God 300 years and had other sons and
daughters. Altogether, Enoch lives a total of 365
years. Enoch walked faithfully with God, and then
he was no more, because God took him away." Now,
you may say that "he was no more, because God took
him away" refers to death, as the verse in
question is a bit vague. Not so.

Enoch was the "seventh from Adam," (Jude 1:14) and
was the great, great, great, great grandson of
Adam and Eve. To locate Enoch's family origins
take a look at Luke 3:37 "The son of Methuselah,
the son of Enoch..." Enoch, the seventh from Adam,
who, at the age of 365, was translated, and went
with God. When Enoch left, only Adam had died,

for the lifespan of 1,000 was still in effect. Noah wasn't born at the time. Enoch is also mention in the Book of Hebrews. The confirmation that he did not die, but was taken can be seen here. Hebrews 11:5 says, "By faith Enoch was taken from this life, so that he did not experience death: 'He could not be found, because God had taken him away' [Genesis 5:24]. For before he was taken, he was commended as one who pleased God."

From this we can gather that Enoch, son of Jared, truly was taken to heaven, just as Elijah was. What have we learned about Enoch? Enoch, a man of faith, lived 365 years (the oldest man who ever lived was Methuselah, Enoch's son, who lived 969 years) and when Enoch was 365, he was removed by God to Heaven.

Now Jude 1:14-15 tells us, "Enoch, the seventh from Adam, prophesied about them: 'See, the Lord is coming with thousands upon thousands of his holy ones to judge everyone, and to convict the ungodly of all the ungodly acts they have done in an ungodly way, and of all the defiant words ungodly sinners have spoken against him.'"

Enoch speaks about how Demons influence mankind. Enoch stated that the sons of God saw the daughters of mankind and took them as their wives. He also accounted that the daughters of man bore children from the sons of God which they bred a new race called the Nephilim. This is referenced in the book of Enoch, chapters 6-14.

1. And it came to pass when the children of men had multiplied that in those days were born unto them beautiful and comely daughters.

2. And the angels, the children of the heaven, saw and lusted after them, and said to one another: 'Come; let us choose us wives from among the children of men

3. and beget us children.' And Semjaza, who was their leader, said unto them: 'I fear ye will not

4. indeed agree to do this deed, and I alone shall have to pay the penalty of a great sin.' And they all answered him and said: 'Let us all swear an oath, and all bind us by mutual imprecations

5. not to abandon this plan but to do this thing.' Then swear they all together and bound themselves

6. by mutual imprecations upon it. And they were in all two hundred; who descended in the days of Jared on the summit of Mount Hermon, and they called it Mount Hermon, because they had sworn

7. and bound themselves by mutual imprecations upon it. And these are the names of their leaders: Samlazaz, their leader, Araklba, Rameel, Kokablel, Tamlel, Ramlel, Danel, Ezeqeel, Baraqijal,

8. Asael, Armaros, Batarel, Ananel, Zaqlel, Samsapeel, Satarel, Turel, Jomjael, Sariel. These are their chiefs of tens.

THE RISE OF THE NEPHILIM (THE FLOOD OF NOAH)

Chapter 7

1. And all the others together with them took unto themselves wives, and each chose for himself one,

and they began to go in unto them and to defile themselves with them, and they taught them charms

2. and enchantments, and the cutting of roots, and made them acquainted with plants. And they

3. became pregnant, and they bare great giants, whose height was three thousand ells: Who consumed

4. all the acquisitions of men. And when men could no longer sustain them, the giants turned against

5. them and devoured mankind. And they began to sin against birds, and beasts, and reptiles, and

6. fish, and to devour one another's flesh, and drink the blood. Then the earth laid accusation against the lawless ones.

Chapter 8

1. And Azazel taught men to make swords, and knives, and shields, and breastplates, and made known to them the metals of the earth and the art of working them, and bracelets, and ornaments, and the use of antimony, and the beautifying of the eyelids, and all kinds of costly stones, and all

2. coloring tinctures. And there arose much godlessness, and they committed fornication, and they

3. were led astray, and became corrupt in all their ways. Semjaza taught enchantments, and root-cuttings, 'Armaros the resolving of enchantments, Baraqijal (taught) astrology, Kokabel the constellations, Ezeqeel the knowledge of the clouds, Araqiel the signs of the earth, Shamsiel the signs of the sun, and Sariel the course of the

moon. And as men perished, they cried, and their cry went up to heaven . . .

Chapter 9

1. And then Michael, Uriel, Raphael, and Gabriel looked down from heaven and saw much blood being

2. shed upon the earth, and all lawlessness being wrought upon the earth. And they said one to another: 'The earth made without inhabitant cries the voice of their cryingst up to the gates of heaven.

3. And now to you, the holy ones of heaven, the souls of men make their suit, saying, "Bring our cause

4. before the Most High."' And they said to the Lord of the ages: 'Lord of lords, God of gods, King of kings, and God of the ages, the throne of Thy glory (standeth) unto all the generations of the

5. ages, and Thy name holy and glorious and blessed unto all the ages! Thou hast made all things, and power over all things hast Thou: and all things are naked and open in Thy sight, and Thou seest all

6. things, and nothing can hide itself from Thee. Thou seest what Azazel hath done, who hath taught all unrighteousness on earth and revealed the eternal secrets which were (preserved) in heaven, which

7. men were striving to learn: And Semjaza, to whom Thou hast given authority to bear rule over his associates. And they have gone to the

daughters of men upon the earth, and have slept with the

9. women, and have defiled themselves, and revealed to them all kinds of sins. And the women have

10. borne giants, and the whole earth has thereby been filled with blood and unrighteousness. And now, behold, the souls of those who have died are crying and making their suit to the gates of heaven, and their lamentations have ascended: and cannot cease because of the lawless deeds which are

11. wrought on the earth. And Thou knowest all things before they come to pass, and Thou seest these things and Thou dost suffer them, and Thou dost not say to us what we are to do to them in regard to these.'

Chapter 10

1. Then said the Most High, the Holy and Great One spake, and sent Uriel to the son of Lamech,

2. and said to him: Go to Noah and tell him in my name "Hide thyself!" and reveal to him the end that is approaching: that the whole earth will be destroyed, and a deluge is about to come

3. upon the whole earth, and will destroy all that is on it. And now instruct him that he may escape

4. and his seed may be preserved for all the generations of the world. And again the Lord said to Raphael: Bind Azazel hand and foot, and cast him into the darkness: and make an opening

5. in the desert, which is in Dudael, and cast him therein. And place upon him rough and jagged rocks, and cover him with darkness, and let him abide there for ever, and cover his face that he may

7. not see light. And on the day of the great judgement he shall be cast into the fire. And heal the earth which the angels have corrupted, and proclaim the healing of the earth, that they may heal the plague, and that all the children of men may not perish through all the secret things that the

8. Watchers have disclosed and have taught their sons. And the whole earth has been corrupted

9. through the works that were taught by Azazel: to him ascribe all sin. And to Gabriel said the Lord: Proceed against the bastards and the reprobates, and against the children of fornication: and destroy [the children of fornication and] the children of the Watchers from amongst men [and cause them to go forth]: send them one against the other that they may destroy each other in

10. battle: for length of days shall they not have. And no request that they (i.e. their fathers) make of thee shall be granted unto their fathers on their behalf; for they hope to live an eternal life, and

11. that each one of them will live five hundred years. And the Lord said unto Michael: Go, bind Semjaza and his associates who have united themselves with women so as to have defiled themselves

12. with them in all their uncleanness. And when their sons have slain one another, and they have seen the destruction of their beloved ones, bind them fast for seventy generations in the valleys of the earth, till the day of their judgement and of their consummation, till the judgement that is

13. forever and ever is consummated. In those days they shall be led off to the abyss of fire: and

14. to the torment and the prison in which they shall be confined forever. And whosoever shall be condemned and destroyed will from thenceforth be bound together with them to the end of all

15. generations. And destroy all the spirits of the reprobate and the children of the Watchers, because

16. they have wronged mankind. Destroy all wrong from the face of the earth and let every evil work come to an end: and let the plant of righteousness and truth appear: and it shall prove a blessing; the works of righteousness and truth shall be planted in truth and joy for evermore.

17. And then shall all the righteous escape, And shall live till they beget thousands of children, and all the days of their youth and their old age shall they complete in peace.

18. And then shall the whole earth be tilled in righteousness, and shall all be planted with trees and

19. be full of blessing. And all desirable trees shall be planted on it, and they shall plant vines on it: and the vine which they plant thereon shall yield wine in abundance, and as for all the seed

which is sown thereon each measure (of it) shall bear a thousand, and each measure of olives shall yield

20. ten presses of oil. And cleanse thou the earth from all oppression, and from all unrighteousness, and from all sin, and from all godlessness: and all the uncleanness that is wrought upon the earth

21. destroy from off the earth. And all the children of men shall become righteous, and all nations

22. shall offer adoration and shall praise me, and all shall worship me. And the earth shall be cleansed from all defilement, and from all sin, and from all punishment, and from all torment, and I will never again send (them) upon it from generation to generation and forever.

Chapter 11

1. And in those days I will open the store chambers of blessing which are in the heaven, so as to send

2. them down upon the earth over the work and labour of the children of men. And truth and peace shall be associated together throughout all the days of the world and throughout all the generations of men.

Chapter 12

1. Before these things Enoch was hidden, and no one of the children of men knew where he was

2. hidden, and where he abode, and what had become of him. And his activities had to do with the Watchers, and his days were with the holy ones.

3. And I Enoch was blessing the Lord of majesty and the King of the ages, and lo! The Watchers

4. called me -Enoch the scribe- and said to me: 'Enoch, thou scribe of righteousness, go, declare to the Watchers of the heaven who have left the high heaven, the holy eternal place, and have defiled themselves with women, and have done as the children of earth do, and have taken unto themselves

5. wives: "Ye have wrought great destruction on the earth: And ye shall have no peace nor forgiveness

6. of sin: and inasmuch as they delight themselves in their children, the murder of their beloved ones shall they see, and over the destruction of their children shall they lament, and shall make supplication unto eternity, but mercy and peace shall ye not attain."

Chapter 13

1. And Enoch went and said: Azazel, thou shalt have no peace: a severe sentence has gone forth

2. against thee to put thee in bonds: And thou shalt not have toleration nor request granted to thee, because of the unrighteousness which thou hast taught, and because of all the works of godlessness

3. and unrighteousness and sin which thou hast shown to men. Then I went and spoke to them all

4. together, and they were all afraid, and fear and trembling seized them. And they besought me to draw up a petition for them that they might find

forgiveness, and to read their petition in the presence

5. of the Lord of heaven. For from thenceforward they could not speak (with Him) nor lift up their

6. eyes to heaven for shame of their sins for which they had been condemned. Then I wrote out their petition, and the prayer in regard to their spirits and their deeds individually and in regard to their

7. requests that they should have forgiveness and length. And I went off and sat down at the waters of Dan, in the land of Dan, to the south of the west of Hermon: I read their petition till I fell and I saw visions of chastisement, and a voice came bidding (me) I to tell to the sons of heaven, and reprimand them.

9. And when I awaked, I came unto them, and they were all sitting gathered together, weeping in

10. Abelsjail, which is between Lebanon and Seneser, with their faces covered. And I recounted before them all the visions which I had seen in sleep, and I began to speak the words of righteousness, and to reprimand the heavenly Watchers.

Chapter 14

1. The book of the words of righteousness, and of the reprimand of the eternal Watchers in accordance

2. with the command of the Holy Great One in that vision. I saw in my sleep what I will now say with a tongue of flesh and with the breath of my mouth: which the Great One has given to men to

3. converse therewith and understand with the heart. As He has created and given to man the power of understanding the word of wisdom, so hath He created me also and given me the power of reprimanding

4. the Watchers, the children of heaven. I wrote out your petition, and in my vision it appeared thus, that your petition will not be granted unto you throughout all the days of eternity, and that judgment

5. has been finally passed upon you: yea (your petition) will not be granted unto you. And from henceforth you shall not ascend into heaven unto all eternity, and in bonds of the earth the decree

6. has gone forth to bind you for all the days of the world. And (that) previously you shall have seen the destruction of your beloved sons and ye shall have no pleasure in them, but they shall fall before

7. you by the sword. And your petition on their behalf shall not be granted, nor yet on your own: even though you weep and pray and speak all the words contained in the writing which I have

8. written. And the vision was shown to me thus: Behold, in the vision clouds invited me and a mist summoned me and the course of the stars and the sped and hastened me, and the winds in

9. the vision caused me to fly and lifted me upward, and bore me into heaven. And I went in till I drew nigh to a wall which is built of crystals and surrounded by tongues of fire: and it began to affright

10. me. And I went into the tongues of fire and drew nigh to a large house which was built of crystals: and the walls of the house were like a tesselated floor (made) of crystals, and its groundwork was

11. of crystal. Its ceiling was like the path of the stars and the lightnings, and between them were

12. fiery cherubim, and their heaven was (clear as) water. A flaming fire the walls, and its

13. portals blazed with fire. And I entered into that house, and it was hot as fire and cold as ice: there

14. were no delights of life therein: fear covered me, and trembling got hold upon me. And as I quaked

15. and trembled, I fell upon my face. And I beheld a vision, And lo! there was a second house, greater

16. than the former, and the entire portal stood open before me, and it was built of flames of fire. And in every respect it so excelled in splendour and magnificence and extent that I cannot describe to

17. you its splendour and its extent. And its floor was of fire, and above it were lightnings and the path

18. of the stars, and its ceiling also was flaming fire. And I looked and saw therein a lofty throne: its appearance was as crystal, and the wheels thereof as the shining sun, and there was the vision of

19. cherubim. And from underneath the throne came streams of flaming fire so that I could not look

20. thereon. And the Great Glory sat thereon, and His raiment shone more brightly than the sun and

21. was whiter than any snow. None of the angels could enter and could behold His face by reason

22. of the magnificence and glory and no flesh could behold Him. The flaming fire was round about Him, and a great fire stood before Him, and none around could draw nigh Him: ten thousand times

23. ten thousand (stood) before Him, yet He needed no counselor. And the most holy ones who were

24. nigh to Him did not leave by night nor depart from Him. And until then I had been prostrate on my face, trembling: and the Lord called me with His own mouth, and said to me: ' Come hither,

25. Enoch, and hear my word.' And one of the holy ones came to me and waked me, and He made me rise up and approach the door: and I bowed my face downwards.

In conclusion there are two separate rebellions from heaven: the rebellion with Lucifer and his followers and the rebellion of the Watchers the Angels that protected the Earth.

The new race the Nephilim were giants of which some stood over 50 feet tall and were destroyed in the flood of Noah. So how do we really know that the Nephilim really existed and is there evidence that can point to the race know as the Nephilim? In order to find the truth, one has to look to the Bible in one story in particular that attest to the Nephilim race - the story of David and

Goliath, which predated the birth of Christ. The story of David and Goliath is one in which a common boy was faced to fight a giant that was nine feet tall. It is possible that Goliath was a descendent of the fallen Angels from heaven. The reference comes from 1 Samuel 17:1-58.

1. Now the Philistines gathered their forces for war and assembled at Sokoh in Judah. They pitched camp at Ephes Dammim, between Sokoh and Azekah.

2. Saul and the Israelites assembled and camped in the Valley of Elah and drew up their battle line to meet the Philistines.

3. The Philistines occupied one hill and the Israelites another, with the valley between them.

4. A champion named Goliath, who was from Gath, came out of the Philistine camp. His height was six cubits and a span.

5. He had a bronze helmet on his head and wore a coat of scale armor of bronze weighing five thousand shekels[b];

6. on his legs he wore bronze greaves, and a bronze javelin was slung on his back.

7. His spear shaft was like a weaver's rod, and its iron point weighed six hundred shekels. [c] His shield bearer went ahead of him.

8. Goliath stood and shouted to the ranks of Israel, "Why do you come out and line up for battle? Am I not a Philistine, and are you not the servants of Saul? Choose a man and have him come down to me.

9. If he is able to fight and kill me, we will become your subjects; but if I overcome him and kill him, you will become our subjects and serve us."

10. Then the Philistine said, "This day I defy the armies of Israel! Give me a man and let us fight each other."

11. On hearing the Philistine's words, Saul and all the Israelites were dismayed and terrified.

12. Now David was the son of an Ephrathite named Jesse, who was from Bethlehem in Judah. Jesse had eight sons, and in Saul's time he was very old.

13. Jesse's three oldest sons had followed Saul to the war: The firstborn was Eliab; the second, Abinadab; and the third, Shammah.

14. David was the youngest. The three oldest followed Saul,

15. but David went back and forth from Saul to tend his father's sheep at Bethlehem.

16. For forty days the Philistine came forward every morning and evening and took his stand.

17. Now Jesse said to his son David, "Take this ephah of roasted grain and these ten loaves of bread for your brothers and hurry to their camp.

18. Take along these ten cheeses to the commander of their unit. See how your brothers are and bring back some assurance from them.

19. They are with Saul and all the men of Israel in the Valley of Elah, fighting against the Philistines."

20. Early in the morning David left the flock in the care of a shepherd, loaded up and set out, as Jesse had directed. He reached the camp as the army was going out to its battle positions, shouting the war cry.

21. Israel and the Philistines were drawing up their lines facing each other.

22. David left his things with the keeper of supplies ran to the battle lines and asked his brothers how they were.

23. As he was talking with them, Goliath, the Philistine champion from Gath, stepped out from his lines and shouted his usual defiance, and David heard it.

24. Whenever the Israelites saw the man, they all fled from him in great fear.

25. Now the Israelites had been saying, "Do you see how this man keeps coming out? He comes out to defy Israel. The king will give great wealth to the man who kills him. He will also give him his daughter in marriage and will exempt his family from taxes in Israel."

26. David asked the men standing near him, "What will be done for the man who kills this Philistine and removes this disgrace from Israel? Who is this uncircumcised Philistine that he should defy the armies of the living God?"

27. They repeated to him what they had been saying and told him, "This is what will be done for the man who kills him."

28. When Eliab, David's oldest brother, heard him speaking with the men, he burned with anger at him

and asked, "Why have you come down here? And with whom did you leave those few sheep in the wilderness? I know how conceited you are and how wicked your heart is; you came down only to watch the battle."

29. "Now what have I done?" said David. "Can't I even speak?"

30. He then turned away to someone else and brought up the same matter, and the men answered him as before.

31. What David said was overheard and reported to Saul, and Saul sent for him.

32. David said to Saul, "Let no one lose heart on account of this Philistine; your servant will go and fight him."

33. Saul replied, "You are not able to go out against this Philistine and fight him; you are only a young man, and he has been a warrior from his youth."

34. But David said to Saul, "Your servant has been keeping his father's sheep. When a lion or a bear came and carried off a sheep from the flock,

35. I went after it, struck it and rescued the sheep from its mouth. When it turned on me, I seized it by its hair, struck it and killed it.

36. Your servant has killed both the lion and the bear; this uncircumcised Philistine will be like one of them, because he has defied the armies of the living God.

37. The LORD who rescued me from the paw of the lion and the paw of the bear will rescue me from

the hand of this Philistine."Saul said to David, "Go, and the LORD be with you."

38. Then Saul dressed David in his own tunic. He put a coat of armor on him and a bronze helmet on his head.

39. David fastened on his sword over the tunic and tried walking around, because he was not used to them. "I cannot go in these," he said to Saul, "because I am not used to them." So he took them off.

40. Then he took his staff in his hand, chose five smooth stones from the stream, put them in the pouch of his shepherd's bag and, with his sling in his hand, approached the Philistine.

41. Meanwhile, the Philistine, with his shield bearer in front of him, kept coming closer to David.

42. He looked David over and saw that he was little more than a boy, glowing with health and handsome, and he despised him.

43. He said to David, "Am I a dog, that you come at me with sticks?" And the Philistine cursed David by his gods.

44. "Come here," he said, "and I'll give your flesh to the birds and the wild animals!"

45. David said to the Philistine, "You come against me with sword and spear and javelin, but I come against you in the name of the LORD Almighty, the of the armies of Israel, whom you have defied.

46. This day the LORD will deliver you into my hands, and I'll strike you down and cut off your

head. This very day I will give the carcasses of the Philistine army to the birds and the wild animals, and the whole world will know that there is a God in Israel.

47. All those gathered here will know that it is not by sword or spear that the LORD saves; for the battle is the LORD's, and he will give all of you into our hands."

48. As the Philistine moved closer to attack him, David ran quickly toward the battle line to meet him.

49. Reaching into his bag and taking out a stone, he slung it and struck the Philistine on the forehead. The stone sank into his forehead, and he fell face down on the ground.

50. So David triumphed over the Philistine with a sling and a stone; without a sword in his hand he struck down the Philistine and killed him.

51. David ran and stood over him. He took hold of the Philistine's sword and drew it from the sheath. After he killed him, he cut off his head with the sword. When the Philistines saw that their hero was dead, they turned and ran.

52. Then the men of Israel and Judah surged forward with a shout and pursued the Philistines to the entrance of Gath[f] and to the gates of Ekron. Their dead were strewn along the Shaaraim road to Gath and Ekron.

53. When the Israelites returned from chasing the Philistines, they plundered their camp.

54. David took the Philistine's head and brought it to Jerusalem; he put the Philistine's weapons in his own tent.

55. As Saul watched David going out to meet the Philistine, he said to Abner, commander of the army, "Abner, whose son is that young man?" Abner replied, "As surely as you live, Your Majesty, I don't know."

56. The king said, "Find out whose son this young man is."

57. As soon as David returned from killing the Philistine, Abner took him and brought him before Saul, with David still holding the Philistine's head.

58. "Whose son are you, young man?" Saul asked him. David said, "I am the son of your servant Jesse of Bethlehem."

Some theologians and scholars dismiss this story implying that the Bible is speaking metaphorically. Is this evidence that the race truly existed? There are skeletal remains of the existence of the Nephilim popping up all over the globe in India and Saudi Arabia. Can the explosion of technology that was acquired at that specific time period attest to the Nephilim?

Chapter 2

ANCIENT EGYPT AND THE PYRAMIDS:
THEIR TRUE PURPOSE

Throughout the reign of the entire Egyptian
civilization one thing that stands out the most to
me is the Pyramid. The Pyramid is one of the
great wonders of the world. These colossal
structures are said to be built by the great
Egyptian race whose rule spanned over 3,000 years
by many different rulers. Ancient Egyptian
religion was a complex system of polytheistic
beliefs and rituals which were an integral part of
ancient Egyptian society. It centered on the
Egyptians' interaction with a multitude of deities
who were believed to be present in, and in control
of, the forces and elements of nature. The myths
about these gods were meant to explain the origins
and behavior of the forces they represented.

The practices of Egyptian religion were efforts to provide for the gods and gain their favor. Formal religious practice centered on the pharaoh, the king of Egypt. Although he was a human, the pharaoh was believed to be descended from the gods. He acted as the intermediary between his people and the gods, and was obligated to sustain the gods through rituals and offerings so that they could maintain order in the universe. Therefore, the state dedicated enormous resources to the performance of these rituals and to the construction of the temples where they were carried out.

Individuals could also interact with the gods for their own purposes, appealing for their help through prayer or compelling them to act through magic. These popular religious practices were distinct from, but closely linked with, the formal rituals and institutions. The popular religious tradition grew more prominent in the course of Egyptian history as the status of the pharaoh declined. Another important aspect of the religion was the belief in the afterlife and funerary practices. The Egyptians made great efforts to ensure the survival of their souls after death, providing tombs, grave goods, and offerings to preserve the bodies and spirits of the deceased.

The religion had its roots in Egypt's prehistory and lasted for more than 3,000 years. The details of religious belief changed over time as the importance of particular gods rose and declined, and their intricate relationships shifted. At various times certain gods became prominent over the others, including the sun god, Ra; the creator god, Amun; and the mother goddess, Isis. For a brief period, in the aberrant theology promulgated by the pharaoh Akhenaten, a single god, the Aten, replaced the traditional pantheon. Yet the overall system endured, even through several periods of foreign rule, until the coming of Christianity in the early centuries AD.

It left behind numerous religious writings and monuments, along with significant influences on cultures both ancient and modern. Perhaps this is evidence that the Pyramids were designed by the Nephilim but labored by human hands. From the accounts of Enoch we know that the Watchers taught man how to make swords, knives, and shields and now possibly the Pyramids. So if you ask most scholars what was the purpose of the Pyramids they would most likely tell you that it was a device to bury the Pharaoh to preserve their bodies for the afterlife. If you would have asked me the same question 20 years ago, I would have told you the exact same thing.

The reason I would say that is because that is what you and I have been lead to believe. Completing research on this gave me a different prospective on where we are as humans in our life cycle. We are in a place and time where we are heavily influenced to do things and believe more in man and less in God. So what is the purpose of the Pyramid? There are many theories about this, but what if it was a transportation vessel? This theory has merit because in 1987 the United States Air Force flew over the Great Pyramid of Giza and it scrambled the airplane instruments.

Further investigation by NASA discovered that the Pyramid emitted a light or an energy beam from the top of the structure. The energy could not be detected by the human eye but by ultra violet rays. The energy beam was actually an energy vortex of swirling particles. What is an energy vortex? It is a swirling pool of energy. So where do the swirling pools of energy go? It's possible that the particles escape space and time only to be captured by another Pyramid in another dimension.

Is it possible that other pyramid are occupied by other Demonic forces in other plans of existence and can only reach our dimension through these Pyramids? When the first rebellion in heaven began is it possible that the Angels were kicked out of the heavens and were scattered all over the universe but possibly in different planes of existence.

The Pyramid is so fascinating because of its size and what types of materials that were used to construct it. It was mostly made out of limestone with some blocks reportedly weighting up to fifty tons. Limestone is a conductor of energy and electricity.

The outer, upper part of the structure has reportedly been removed by looters and earthquakes. Is it possible that the materials were removed by followers of some secret societies only to be restored in the most opportune moment? So what is the opportune moment for the materials to be placed again? Upon further research I began to see that the Pyramid structure was used in other parts of the world, in civilizations like the Aztec, Maya and Chinese cultures.

THE MAYA CIVILIZATION AND THE CONTINUANCE OF DEMONIC RITUALS

The materials used to build the Pyramids were common to the area in which they were constructed. Say for instance in Egypt they used limestone whereas in China they used mud and dirt. So the materials used depended on what was in the local area of the structure. To discover the opportune time in which it needed to be placed, I looked at the Maya Civilization. Early records of the Maya Civilization date back to 2000 BC. By all accounts the Mayas were advanced among our wildest dreams.

One thing that has set them apart from all other civilizations was their ability to foresee the future or to forecast the future. The Mayas did not predict the end of the world; however, their long calendar ends on December 2012, which leaves many to speculate why it ended. The time in which the calendar ends is December 21, 2012. Some theories out there are the belief that our planet, moon, sun, and galaxy would be in perfect alignment with each other. This is said to cause our sun to release large amounts of gamma rays to strike our planet causing the end of our world. Other scientists believe in geomagnetic reversal or change in the Earth's magnetic field such that the positions of magnetic north and magnetic south are interchanged.

Is it possible that the alignment is like a doorway to our dimension and on that day it will be opened allowing these demonic sprits into our plane of existence. No one knows what will exactly happen but the chances for demonic spirits being let into our dimension should be considered. The possibility of these things accruing is through the Pyramids. So what was explained is how all

this started and by who. But now let focus on the
government and what effect it has on you and your
everyday life.

GOVERNMENT: THE CREATION OF COMMUNISM AND
DEMOCRATIC SYSTEMS

When I began my research I wanted to know where
the first governmental system started from. I
found that the Egyptian system was Communist in
nature. Communism is a movement to create a
classless, moneyless, stateless social order
structured upon common ownership of the means of
production, as well as a social, political and
economic ideology that aims at the establishment
of this social order. This movement, in its
Marxist-Leninist interpretations, significantly
influenced the history of the 20th century, which
saw intense rivalry between the "socialist world"
(socialist states ruled by Communist parties) and
the "western world" (countries with market
economies), culminating in the Cold War between
the Eastern bloc and the "Free World." Essentially
Communism is a governmental system set under the
leadership of one person or a group of people.

Joseph Stalin was one of the most ruthless leaders
in Russian history and continues to receive much
criticism. Stalin's rule spanned from 1922 until
his death in 1953, during which time he had a
great impact on his country. It has been estimated
that Stalin was responsible for more than
20,000,000 deaths during his reign. Considering
that Stalin died in 1953, note what Conquest did
not include -- camp deaths after 1950, and before
1936; executions 1939-53; the vast deportation of
the people of captive nations into the camps, and

their deaths 1939-1953; the massive deportation within the Soviet Union of minorities 1941-1944; and their deaths; and those the Soviet Red Army and secret police executed throughout Eastern Europe after their conquest during 1944-1945. Moreover, omitted is the deadly Ukrainian famine Stalin purposely imposed on the region and that killed 5,000,000 in 1932-1934.

So, Conquest's estimates are spotty and incomplete. That estimate is very conservative; in fact it has been re-estimated the Stalin may have been responsible for more than 60,000,000 deaths. So a more realistic number would be 20,000,000 to 60,000,000. The list of Communist countries includes Russia, China, North Korea and Cuba just to name a few. Communist systems seem to ignore the rights of the common people it seeks to rule.

The Egyptian government belief system was based on gods and not one God. Is it possible that government was formed by demons or, to be precise, the Nephilim (the offspring of the fallen Angles and the daughters of mankind)? It was a means if controlling all of its inhabitants under one system. The opposite of Communism is a Democracy and a Democracy is defined as an egalitarian form of government in which all the citizens of a nation together determine public policy, the laws and the actions of their state, requiring that all citizens (meeting certain qualifications) have an equal opportunity to express their opinion. In practice, "Democracy" is the extent to which a given system approximates this ideal, and a given political system is referred to as "a democracy" if it allows a certain approximation to ideal democracy. Although no country has ever granted

all its citizens (i.e. including minors) the right
to vote, most countries today hold regular
elections based on egalitarian principles, at
least in theory.

The most common system that is deemed "democratic"
in the modern world is parliamentary democracy in
which the voting public takes part in elections
and chooses politicians to represent them in a
Legislative Assembly. The members of the assembly
then make decisions with a majority vote. A purer
form is direct democracy in which the voting
public makes direct decisions or participates
directly in the political process. Elements of
direct democracy exist on a local level and on a
national level in many countries, though these
systems coexist with representative assemblies.
The term comes from the Greek word d.μ...at.a
(demokratía) "rule of the people", which was
coined from d.μ... (Demos) "People" and ...t...
(kratos) "Power" in the middle of the 5th-4th
century BC to denote the political systems then
existing in some Greek city-states, notably Athens
following a popular uprising in 508 BC. Other
cultures since Greece have significantly
contributed to the evolution of democracy such as
Ancient Rome, Europe, and North and South America.

CAN A DEMOCRACY LED TO COMMUNISM?

In a Democracy the group favors or targets the
middle or lower class citizens. Can this type of
government system be dangerous? In this type of
governmental system the public have a say in what
direction the country should go. One of the

earliest documents of Democratic systems has its formal origins in Ancient Greece, but democratic practices are evident in earlier societies including Mesopotamia, Phoenicia, and India. A republic is a form of government in which the government is officially apportioned to the control of the people, or a significant portion of which, and where offices of state are subsequently directly or indirectly elected or appointed.

In modern times, a common simplified definition of a republic is a government where the head of state is NOT a monarch. The word republic is derived from the Latin phrase res publica, which can be translated as "the public affair," and often used to describe a state using this form of government. In a Republican system the people with the power and influence have more of a say on how the government should be run. In a Republican government there is election rigging and deals being made behind closed doors without the knowledge and consent of the people. In early civilization you can see that politics affected the course of history.

When the SYSTEM began it began on the ground floor and this how politics affected everything. Imagine building a house from the ground up and while you are building it you put in place certain tools or doors that are hidden that allows you access to any part of the house. Thus allowing you to be wherever you want to be giving you the opportunity to make changes where and when you deemed necessary. During the reign of the Roman Empire you had the emergence of Christianity. Christianity is the belief that there is one Supreme Being, God. During the Roman Empire came the birth of Christ who died for everyone's sin, because when Adam and Eve ate from the tree of knowledge they sinned for all generations to come.

THE ROMAN EMPIRE AND JESUS CHRIST

But God had a divine plan before the creation of man as seen in the birth of Christ. Without the death and resurrection of Christ, there would be no redemption for the sins that Adam and Eve passed on to us all. Since the creation of mankind there has been demonic influence. As Christ grew from a boy to a man there was demonic influence. The story of Jesus and his apostles tells many stories of Jesus and his disciples casting out Demons.

Mark 1:23-27 Now there was a man in their synagogue with an unclean spirit. And he cried out, saying, "Let us alone! What have we to do with You, Jesus of Nazareth? Did you come to destroy us? I know who You are --the Holy One of God!" But Jesus rebuked him, saying, "Be quiet, and come out of him!" And when the unclean spirit had convulsed him and cried out with a loud voice, he came out of him. Then they were all amazed, so that they questioned among themselves, saying, "What is this? What new doctrine is this? For with authority He [Jesus] commands even the unclean spirits, and they obey Him."

A Hollywood depiction of this is displayed in the movie The Passion of the Christ. Peter was influenced by Demons to betray Jesus to the Romans which was a combination of influences. If Peter was not influenced would we have redemption now?

That attests to the mighty and divine power of God. Only God could have known that this would happen. The death and resurrection of Christ was the beginning of the fall of this great Empire.

There were six world empires.

1. Egypt 1400 BC under the Pharaohs

2. Assyria 1000 BC under Sennacherib

3. Babylon 1000 BC under Nebuchadnezzar

4. Medo Persia 606-583 BC

5. Macedonia or Greece

6. Rome (Holy Roman Empire broke in pieces) 44 BC 177 AD Under Caesar

7. The Revived Roman Empire

After the fall of the Roman Empire came the emergence of religion and the Roman Catholic Church. Catholic doctrine teaches that the Roman Catholic Church was founded by Jesus Christ at the Confession of Peter. It interprets the Confession of Peter as acknowledging Christ's designation of Apostle Peter and his successor to be the temporal head of his Church. Thus, it asserts that the Bishop of Rome has the sole legitimate claim to Petrine authority and the primacy due to the Roman Pontiff. The Catholic Church claims legitimacy for its bishops and priests via the doctrine of apostolic succession and authority of the Pope via the unbroken line of popes, claimed as successors to Simon Peter.

The Roman Catholic Church saw that Man's radical views were not in the nature of God and the Church. The Church knew that there were certain people and groups that did not appeal to the direction of God and the Church. So the church began to seek and destroy these influences.

Chapter 3

The Rise of Secret Societies Which May Be Demonic in Nature

THE ILLUMINATI

One of the groups that the church viewed as radical was the Illuminati. The name is given to several groups that are real and made up. The group was founded in 1771 under the name the Bavarian Illuminati an Enlightenment-era secret society. The name refers to an elite group or conspiratorial organization which tries to create a New World Order in which it controls all of man-kind. The Illuminati in this context is usually represented as a modern version of the Bavarian Illuminati.

Jesuit-taught Adam Weishaupt, who was the first law professor on canon law at the University of Ingolstadt, founded the movement on May 1, 1776 in

Ingolstadt as the Order of the Illuminati with five initial members. It is said it was modeled by the Freemasons made of freethinkers as an offshoot of enlightenment. Every member took a vow of secrecy and a pledge of obedience to their superiors. Many Illuminati chapters drew membership from existing Masonic lodges in which members were divided into their main classes, each with several degrees. The order was originally planned to be name the "Perfectibilist."

The Bavarian Illuminati is another name and its ideology has been named "Illuminism." Brunswick and Von Zwack counted themselves as members holding high positions within the order. In the European countries the order had more than 2000 members over a ten year span. It also attracted Johann Wolfgang von Goethe and Johann Gottfried Herder. Karl Theodor who took rule in 1777 in Bavaria banned all secret societies including the Illuminati because he had a disposition against the Enlightenment movement.

Panic over succession led to its downfall which was affected by the Secular Edict. The blow that really brought the Illuminati in Bavaria to its knees was the March 2, 1785, edict. Weishaupt vanished and internal correspondences and documents were seized and published by the government in 1787. Much of the group's literature was captured when they searched Von Zwack's home. In 1780 after the Lower Saxon noble Adolph Freihrr Knigge joined the Illuminati it went under reorganization, and when it was complete it resembled the Freemasons.

Due to the design of the organization it allowed Freemasons to be recruited in the backdrop of a crisis that the German Freemasons were going through. This claimed succession from the Knights Templars and helped Karl Gotthelf von Hund get the German lodges under his control. At the time he was claiming to be the contact of Unknown Superiors who had given him knowledge of what Freemasonry was all about. After Hund's death no superiors contacted the lodge, leaving the members confused. The most radical proponents of the Enlightenment, Knigge and Franz Dietrich von Ditfurth claimed the opinion leadership for their order in 1782 in early September at the Freemasons Convent of the Strict Observance.

The Order of Strict Observance remained in minority after the templar system was given up. Johann Christoph Bode, the leading representative of the Strict Observance, was overwhelmed by the Illuminati. The disagreements between the two different groups threatened to break up the order in 1784 in a tribunal called a Congress to solve the disagreement of the two parties. What was agreed upon was that the two heads of the Order should resign from their positions of power. After all was said and done, Knigge left the Illuminati in 1784. While members were still quarrelling with each other they attracted the attention of the Bavarian authorities.

The authorities saw the order as radical and a danger to society as they knew it. Prince Charles Theodore banned any communities from conducting private meetings without his approval in 1784. An edict was released in March of 1785 naming members of the Freemasons and the Illuminati. During this time there were house raids and evidence proving their radical views were confiscated. The documents found gave information about several key members. One of the members that were implicated was Pope Pius VI - membership was deemed not compatible with the Catholic faith.

The Illuminati's moral system, supposedly their most valuable secret, was practiced inside the order but not in the outside world. Disagreements within the lower order were caused by Weishaupt's aim to convert members to a more directive position in the order. His goal was to improve the individual by giving knowledge about its secrets. The Illuminati mainly was comprised of subordinate academics, the majority of which joined in the hope of boosting their career opportunities. This correlated with Weishaupt's concept of infiltration.

Through the years there have been many books written about the Illuminati that are viewed as conspiracy theories. Some of these books gained great attention due to the secrecy of the Order. Many of these books claim that world events have been shaped by the Illuminati. Whatever the case, there is too much information about the Illuminati to just leave it up to chance. There are also conspiracy theories that implicate the Illuminati infiltration of Hollywood and the film industry.

THE BILDERBURGS

Another very influential known secret society is the Bilderbers. The Bilderberg Club or The Bilderberg Group hosts an invitation-only

conference that consists of 100 to 160 guests from
Western Europe and North America that meet once a
year. These guests come from backgrounds in
education, communication, finance, labor, politics
and government, and the meetings are closed to the
public. The first conference was held in 1954 at
the Hotel de Bilderberg in the Netherlands. The
conference was created so that leaders from
countries such as the United States and Europe
could be brought together to promote cooperation
and gain a better understanding of each country's
economic political and defense issues.

Prince Bernhard of the Netherlands was approached
by Retinger from Poland who agreed to support the
idea with the head of Unilever, Dutchman Paul
Rijkens, and former Belgian Prime Minister, Paul
Van Zeeland. Also, head of the CIA, Walter
Bedell Smith, and Charles Douglas Jackson were
contacted by Bernhard and invited to attend.
There were two guests from each nation: one
representing a liberal viewpoint and the other a
conservative viewpoint. The first conference
consisted of a total of 61 guests with 50 guests
from 11 Western European countries and with 11
Americans.

The conference was such a success that it led to
annual meeting with Retinger acting as the
permanent secretary of the Steering Committee.
The committee created an informal network of
attendee's names and contact information so
individuals could contact each other in a private
setting. The first three annual meetings took
place in Germany, France, and Denmark. The Ford
Foundation funded the first conference in the

United States in 1957 in St. Simons, Georgia, and also funded conferences in 1959 and 1963. Many professors and skeptics believe that the meetings coincide with world events.

Peter Thompson, a researcher who wrote a book in 1980 titled <u>Bilderberg and the West</u>, states that the group is a meeting place were political figures and top executives from the world's top corporations meet and discuss short- and long-term issues of the Western countries. Thompson stated that the Bilderberg is a group were all it members have a say in how the world should be shaped and have enormous amounts of resources to accomplish whatever agenda they wish to push. Their agreement on how the change should occur is not always in line with the group's long-term strategy. The Steering Committee organizes the meeting with two members from each nation. The only category that exists in the group is the members of the Steering Committee.

In 1960 Ernst van der Beugel became the permanent secretary. In 2008 a press release from the Bilderberg stated that the group was only active once a year. It also mentioned the names of the attendees. The official headquarters for the group is located in the Netherlands. In 2008 the agenda dealt with cyber terrorism, Russia, Africa, Afghanistan, Iran, and Islam.

Past attendee lists lean more to bankers and politicians and North American corporations including IBM, Xerox, and Nokia. In 2009 the meeting included Greek Prime Minister, Kostas Karamanlis, and a few key figures from the Netherlands. The meeting was hosted in Brussels at the castle of the Valley of the Duchess. It was stated in the 1950 that the Western countries grew concerned that the United Nations was not controlled by Western powers.

In 1977 Sklar quoted from human rights journalist Caroline Moorehead that "No invitations go out to representatives of the developing countries; otherwise you turn into a mini United Nation." The group seeks like-minded and compatible people. Moorehead pictures the group as heavily biased to politics and big business. When the meetings are held there is private security in conjunction with local police authorities. News organizations attempting to cover the event have reported being subjected to reprisals. There have been many cases of reporters being arrested for taking pictures or attempting to gain access to the conference.

What makes these meetings so important is that the attendees can speak openly without scrutiny from the media or the general public. The group is accused of conspiracies such as trying to form a world government through politics and large corporations. Proponents of the conspiracy theories in the United States include the John Birch Society, Alex Jones, and politician Jesse Ventura. In 2001 a Bilderberg member name Denis Healey was quoted, "To say we were striving for a one world government is exaggerated, but not wholly unfair. Those of us in Bilderberg felt we couldn't go on forever fighting one another and killing people and rendering millions homeless. So we felt that a single community throughout the world would be a good thing." In 2005 Davignon discussed these accusations with the BBC and he down played the comments by saying, "If we were a secret government of the world we should be bloody ashamed of ourselves." Author James McConnachie stated that the conspiracy theorists have a point, but they fail to communicate it effectively. He also states that the group acts in a manner that is consistent with global domination.

FREEMASONRY

The most prominent of these groups were the Freemasons, whose overall objective was to setup the New World Order under the direction of the Illuminati. The groups started out on the ground from how they wanted the country to be shaped. The New World was the term that was coined by the Florentine explorer Amerigo Vespucci which described the Western Hemisphere, specifically America. The term originated in the 16th century, shortly after America was discovered by European explores. The United States of America started off with a belief in God and that everyone could have freedom.

The first explorer was said to be Christopher Columbus but there had been inhabitants living here for years before Christopher Columbus came. We all know this because the Native Americans are still receiving money and grants for what we, the United States of America, have done to them. When the United States was formed, how is it that some of the founding fathers belonged to these secret societies? Some of the founding members were Freemasons. It is said that the Freemasons began as a fraternal organization which started in the late 16th century to early 17th century. Freemasonry now exists in various forms all over the world, with a membership estimated at around six million, including approximately 150,000 under the jurisdictions of the Grand Lodge of Scotland and Grand Lodge of Ireland, over a quarter of a million under the jurisdiction of the United Grand Lodge of England and just under two million in the United States.

The fraternity is administratively organized into independent Grand Lodges or sometimes Orients, each of which governs its own jurisdiction, which consists of subordinate (or constituent) Lodges. The various Grand Lodges recognize each other, or not, based upon adherence to landmarks (a Grand Lodge will usually deem other Grand Lodges who share common landmarks to be regular, and those that do not to be "irregular" or "clandestine"). There are also appending bodies, which are organizations related to the main branch of Freemasonry, but with their own independent administration. The origins and early development of Freemasonry are a matter of some debate and conjecture. A poem known as the "Regius Manuscript" has been dated to approximately 1390 and is the oldest known Masonic text.

There is evidence to suggest that there were Masonic lodges in existence in Scotland as early as the late 16th century (for example the Lodge at Kilwinning, Scotland, has records that date to the late 16th century, and is mentioned in the Second Schaw Statutes (1599). What or whom the Freemasons worship, is a source of much speculation. Over the years, some people have claimed that Freemasons worship Lucifer, or Satan. The truth of the matter is that the name Lucifer is not found in the

rituals of the Blue Lodge, or the York Rite. We do
not believe that Lucifer is mentioned by name in
the Scottish Rite degrees, either.

However, one of the "Sacred Words" in the 17th
Degree of the Scottish Rite is "Abaddon," the
angel of the bottomless pit, mentioned in
Revelation 9:11. Worship does occur in Masonic
Lodges. One of the primary purposes of Freemasonry
is worship. That fact is clearly stated in the
Declaration of Principles which is contained on
pages 37-39 of the Indiana Monitor and Freemason's
Guide. (To examine the source materials, see
footnotes.) Masons worship a god which they call
the Great Architect of the Universe. The symbol
they have chosen to represent their god is the All
Seeing Eye, which the Egyptians used to represent
their pagan god, Osiris.

Many Masons are well aware of the pagan
connection. It is clearly stated in a number of
Masonic Monitors. An example is found on page 116
of the Kentucky Monitor. Since Freemasonry teaches
a false plan of salvation, Masons are not
following in the teachings of Jesus Christ. 2 John
1:9 allows us to know that since they are not
following in the teachings of Jesus, they do not
have God. Freemasonry is classic paganism. 1
Corinthians 10:20-21 allows us to know that the
sacrifices of pagans are offered to demons, rather
than God. Although we can say with certainty that
the god of Freemasonry is a demon, we do not know
specifically which demon Masons worship in lodge.
We simply know that they refer to their demon as
the Great Architect of the Universe, or GAOTU.

All demons are under the leadership of Satan. Therefore, Freemasons cannot avoid worshiping Satan by proxy. Very few of them realize the facts in this aspect of Masonic worship. A great many Masons, even some who do not claim to be Christians, would leave the lodge immediately if the names of Satan, or Lucifer, were substituted for the GAOTU in Masonic prayers. Satan would not allow that to occur, because the more effective the lie is the one which is closer to the truth, without being true. The reason that a name such as the GAOTU is chosen for the object of worship is discussed in The Men's Club, an essay on the Ex-Masons for Jesus website.

There are clear references to the existence of lodges in England by the mid-17th century. The fact that this organization is kept secret could attest to the belief that it origins go back further. It has traces that can be seen hundreds of years ago dating back to the Egyptians and Mayans. Is it possible that the Illuminati use Astrology rituals and symbolism which can be seen as demonic? Freemasons believe in a supreme being but this in itself is deceptive. One of the greatest Freemason of all-time is Albert Pike. Pike was born on December 29, 1809, in Boston the oldest of six children of Benjamin and Sara Pike.

Pike graduated from Harvard and served as a General in the Confederate Army. Pike was found guilty of treason and pardoned by fellow Freemason President Andrew Johnson in 1866. In 1867 Pike received his 32nd Freemasonry degree from the Scottish Rite officials. Pike was fluent in up to 16 different languages and could read and write in all of them; some people believed he was a genius. Pike was one of the founding fathers and the head of the Ancient Accepted Scottish Rite of Freemasonry when he received his 33rd degree and also was the Grand Commander of North American Freemasonry from 1859 to 1891.

The Knights for the Ku Klux Klan made him a top leader in 1869. A Satanist who indulged in the occult, Pike was said to be in constant communication with the Lucifer. In 1737 a group known as the Order of the Palladium made him the Grand Master. There is a statue of Pike in Washington D.C., making him the only Confederate general to have a statue on federal property. The statue was proposed to be removed by Lyndon H. Barouche during the 1992 presidential campaign; he subsequently suffered attacks from Freemasons.

In 1834 an Italian by the name of Giusseppe Mazzini a 33rd degree Mason was selected by the Illuminati to lead their world operations. In 1860 Mazzini founded the notorious Mafia. As the Bavarian government cracked down on secret societies and the Illuminati, the group began to disband only to pop up in other similar organizations like the Freemasons. Mazzini persuaded Albert Pike to the Illuminati. The idea of a one world government fascinated Pike, and he was asked by Mazzini to write a ritual that guided top-ranking masons into top-ranking Illuminati masons. Mazzini also felt that Pike was capable of heading up the Illuminati's American chapter. Once the Mason had made his way up the ladder of Freemasonry and proved to be worthy, only then would he be offered membership to the secret society within the society. Most Freemasons openly deny that their organization has evil intentions or worship the devil but the majority of

Freemasons never reach the 30th degree, therefore, they would never know that they, in fact, worship Lucifer.

One personal occasion that I can attest to this is when I was in the Armed Forces. I was stationed overseas in a foreign country. There was this high ranking superior (Mr. M) that was located in the same unit I was in. Mr. M was a high-ranking Freemason but was not living the life of a Freemason or a Christian. Years passed by and I was relocated to another duty station. I was shopping and saw Mr. M and began speaking with him. He looked very different and was in great health.

As we kept talking I could see that he had God within him. I asked about his involvement with Freemasonry and he said that he left the order. I asked why and he asked if I knew he was a high-ranking member; I said yes. He said that they worship the devil and my mind was blown, but I could not say anything. He said that he was in a ceremony which he was receiving the highest degree when he was made aware of their evil intentions. He told me that since then he had turned his life over to God. He said he would not go into further details because he feared that his life would be in danger. What he could tell me is that I should look for this book written by a high ranking Freemason, but I can't recall of the name. At the time I didn't believe him but now, that's a different story. But here is a letter dated January 22, 1870, from Mazzini to Pike:

"We must allow all the federations to continue just as they are, with their systems, their central authorities and their diverse modes of correspondence between high grades of the same rite, organized as they are at the present, but we must create a super rite, which will remain unknown, to which we will call those Masons of high degree whom we shall select. With regard to our brothers in Masonry, these men must be pledged to the strictest secrecy. Through this supreme rite, we will govern all Freemasonry which will become the one international center, the more powerful because its direction will be unknown."

Keep in mind that Freemasonry was infiltrated by the Illuminati who were looking for a place to hide their true purpose. After Mazzini's death in 1872 Pike appointed Adriano Lemmi, a 33rd degree Mason and banker from Italy, to head the group activities in Europe. Lemmi was a great choice because he was an active member of the Luciferian Society which was founded by Pike and was a supporter of revolutionary Giuseppe Garibaldi. Lemmi was succeeded by Lenin and Lenin was succeeded by Trotsky and Trotsky was succeeded by Stalin. All of these men were backed by American, German, and French banks that were controlled by the House of Rothschild. In a letter written in 1871 by Albert Pike to Mazzini, Pike described in detail plans for three world wars which he had a dream about. During this time Pike drew a military blueprint for these three world wars which ended in a final war sometime in the 20th Century which would bring about the One World Order. The branches that Albert Pike established were the Supreme Council I Charleston, South Carolina, North America, Africa, Asia, Europe, South America and 23 subordinate councils in various places throughout the world. There is no conclusive proof that the letter really existed but here is an excerpt of the letter showing how the three world wars have been planned for many years.

"The First World War must be brought about in order to permit the Illuminati to overthrow the power of the Czars in Russia and of making that country a fortress of atheistic Communism. The divergences caused by the 'agentur' (agents) of the Illuminati between the British and Germanic Empires will be used to foment this war. At the end of the war, Communism will be built and used in order to destroy the other governments and in order to weaken the religions."

"The Second World War must be fomented by taking advantage of the differences between the Fascists and the political Zionists. This war must be brought about so that Nazism is destroyed and that the political Zionism be strong enough to institute a sovereign state of Israel in Palestine. During the Second World War, International Communism must become strong enough in order to balance Christendom, which would be then restrained and held in check until the time when we would need it for the final social cataclysm."

"The Third World War must be fomented by taking advantage of the differences caused by the 'agentur' of the Illuminati between the political Zionists and the leaders of Islamic World. The war must be conducted in such a way that Islam (the Muslim Arabic World) and political Zionism (the State of Israel) mutually destroy each other. Meanwhile the other nations, once more divided on this issue will be constrained to fight to the point of complete physical, moral, spiritual and economical exhaustion…We shall unleash the Nihilists and the atheists, and we shall provoke a formidable social cataclysm which in all its horror will show clearly to the nations the effect of absolute atheism, origin of savagery and of the most bloody turmoil. Then everywhere, the citizens, obliged to defend themselves against the world minority of revolutionaries, will exterminate those destroyers of civilization, and the multitude, disillusioned with Christianity, whose deistic spirits will from that moment be without compass or direction, anxious for an ideal, but without knowing where to render its adoration, will receive the true light through the universal manifestation of the pure doctrine of Lucifer, brought finally out in the public view. This manifestation will result from the general reactionary movement which will follow the destruction of Christianity and atheism, both conquered and exterminated at the same time." [4]

Since the September 11, 2001, attacks there has been instability in the Arabic community and modern Zionism. Is this in order with the coming of a third world war?

It is seen here that Albert Pike was a very influential person in the order but where else can his influence be seen?

THE KKK A DIVERSION BY THE ILLUMINATI

It is said that Pike was also a member of the KKK so who are the KKK? The KKK or the Ku Klux Klan is a group organized in the United State that pushes extremist white supremacy, white nationalism, and anti-immigration through terrorism. It is classified as a hate group and is estimated to have over 5,000 members to this day. The KKK formed in the early 1860s in the southern part of the United States. They are known for their white robes, masks, and conical hats which hide their true identities.

The KKK flourished in the 1920s claiming nationwide status by burning crosses and has well documented records of engaging in terrorism and political violence. The group was founded in 1865 in Pulaski, Tennessee, by six veterans of the Confederate Army. During the Reconstruction era in the United States, the Klan swept through the South as an insurgent movement. The Klan targeted blacks with violence and murder; this led the federal government to pass of the Force Acts, which was used to prosecute crimes that the Klan committed.

In 1921 the group adopted a modern business plan for recruiting and grew nationwide. The group preached One Hundred Percent Americanism and called for better enforcement of prohibition. Most of the violence was generated in the South where some local groups took part in violent attacks on private homes and cross burning. In the 1920s the group was at its peak in which it was said to have well over four to five million members. Criminal behavior by its leaders led to the decline in membership which dropped to 30,000 by 1930. Today the group is considered as a terrorist organization. In 1999 the city council of Charleston, South Carolina, passed a resolution declaring the Klan to be a terrorist organization.

The Klan is seen by some conspiracy theorists as a diversion established by Albert Pike, who began and chose the direction of the Klan. It is said that the Klan's purpose was to divert suspicion from the Illuminati and the Freemasons so that their plans for world control would go undetected.

WANTS AND NEEDS:

WHAT CONNECTS US TO EVERYTHING

One of the things that connect us with everything is desire! When I say desire I mean what we want versus what we need as human beings. All the things that we will ever need have already been provided by God. But what we want is something that we don't have to have, but is unnecessary for survival. Say for instance you have a beautiful home, car, and a 40-inch TV, but a newer model just came out. That is something you don't need but you want. Now on the other hand you have a need and that is imperative to your survival – like needing adequate food and water to survive. So this is something that you actually need.

MONEY: WAS IT CREATED TO CONTROL YOU?

When you understand the basis of what makes something work, you can then control it.

Man would seem to believe that he has had a hard life so in order to make things easier for himself, certain inventions came about in order to make life much easier. Such was the invention of the concept of currency or money, which connects everyone, everywhere. Money is any object or record that is generally accepted as payment for goods and services and repayment of debts in a given country or socio-economic context. The main functions of money are distinguished as: a medium of exchange; a unit of accounting; a store of value; and, occasionally in the past, a standard of deferred payment.

Any kind of object or secure verifiable record that fulfills these functions can serve as money. Money originated as commodity money, but nearly all contemporary money systems are based on fiat money. Fiat money is without intrinsic use value as a physical commodity, and derives its value by being declared by a government to be legal tender; that is, it must be accepted as a form of payment within the boundaries of the country, for "all debts, public and private." The money supply of a country consists of currency (banknotes and coins) and bank money (the balance held in checking accounts and savings accounts). Bank money usually forms by far the largest part of the money supply.

Money comes in many forms and shapes but most all countries have their own money but on January 1, 1999, the European Union consolidated all the money under this one system and created the Euro. The euro (Greek: ...., Evró) (sign: €; code: EUR) is the official currency of the euro zone: 17 of the 27 member states of the European Union. It is also the currency used by the Institutions of the European Union. The euro zone consists of Austria,

Belgium, Cyprus, Estonia, Finland, France, Germany, Greece, Ireland, Italy, Luxembourg, Malta, the Netherlands, Portugal, Slovakia, Slovenia, and Spain.

The currency is also used in five additional European countries and consequently used daily by some 332 million Europeans. Additionally, over 175 million people worldwide - including 150 million people in Africa - use currencies which are pegged to the euro. The euro is the second largest reserve currency as well as the second most traded currency in the world after the United States dollar. As of February 2012, with more than €890 billion in circulation, the euro has the highest combined value of banknotes and coins in circulation in the world, having surpassed the US dollar. Based on International Monetary Fund estimates of 2008 GDP and purchasing power parity among the various currencies, the euro zone is the second largest economy in the world.

PETROLEUM: WHAT MAKES YOU A SLAVE TO THE SYSTEM?

Everyone knows what petroleum is - you have used it and are still using it today.   It is the one thing that drives the economy and effects it like nothing else does around the globe. Petroleum in one form or another, has been used since ancient times and is now important across society, including in economy, politics, and technology. The rise in importance was mostly due to the invention of the internal combustion engine, the rise in commercial aviation, and the increasing use of plastic. More than 4,000 years ago, according to Herodotus and Diodorus Siculus, asphalt was used in the construction of the walls and towers of Babylon (there were oil pits near Ardericca and a pitch spring in Zacynthus).

Great quantities of it were found on the banks of the river Issus, one of the tributaries of the Euphrates. Ancient Persian tablets indicate the medicinal and lighting uses of petroleum in the upper levels of their society. By AD 347, oil was produced for bamboo-drilled wells in China. Access to oil was and still is a major factor in several military conflicts of the twentieth century, including World War II, during which oil facilities were major strategic assets and were extensively bombed. Operation Barbarossa included the goal to capture the Baku oilfields, as it would provide much needed oil supplies for the German military which was suffering from blockades.

Oil exploration in North America during the early 20th century led to the U.S. becoming the leading producer by the mid 1900s. As petroleum production in the U.S. peaked during the 1960s, however, the United States was surpassed by Saudi Arabia and Russia. Today about 90% of vehicular fuel needs are met by oil. Petroleum also makes up 40% of total energy consumption in the United States, but is responsible for only 1% of electricity generation. Petroleum's worth as portable, dense energy source powering that vast majority of vehicles and as the base of many industrial chemicals makes it one of the world's most important commodities.

Viability of the oil commodity is controlled by sever key parameters, number of vehicles in the world competing for fuel, quantity of oil exported to the world competing for fuel, quantity of oil exported to the world market, net energy gain (useful energy provided minus energy consumed), political stability of oil exporting nations, and ability to defend oil supply lines. The three oil producing countries are Saudi Arabia, Russia, and the United States. About 80% of the world's readily accessible reserves are located in the Middle East, with 62.5% coming from Saudi Arabia, UAE, Iraq, Qatar, and Kuwait. A large portion of the world's total oil exists as unconventional sources, such as bitumen in Canada and Venezuela and oil shale. While significant volumes of oil are extracted from oil sands, particularly in Canada, logistical and technical hurdles remain, as oil extraction requires large amounts of heat and water, making its net energy content quite low relative to conventional crude oil.

Thus Canada's oil sands are not expected to provide more than a few million barrels per day in the foreseeable future. Extracting and producing oil can be very dangerous and have made irreversible impacts on our daily lives. Let's take a look at how it affects wildlife: the oil penetrates into the structure of the plumage of birds and animals, reducing its insulating ability, thus making the birds more vulnerable to temperature fluctuations and much less buoyant in the water. Because oil floats on top of water, less sunlight penetrates into the water, limiting the photosynthesis of marine plants and phytoplankton.

There are three kinds of oil-consuming bacteria. Sulfate-reducing bacteria and acid-producing bacteria are anaerobic which general aerobic bacteria are anaerobic. Cleanup and recovery from an oil spill is difficult and depends upon many factors, including the type of oil spilled, the temperature of the water and the types of shorelines and beaches involved. One that has had a direct impact on the U.S. is the Deepwater Horizon oil spill or the BP oil spill. The BP oil spill flowed for three months in 2010 and is the largest accidental marine oil spill in the history of the petroleum industry.

The spill stemmed from a sea floor oil gusher that resulted from the April 20, 2010, explosion of Deepwater Horizon, which drilled on the BP operated Macondo Prospect. The explosion killed 11 men working on the platform and injured 17 others. On July 15, 2010, the leak was stopped by capping the gushing wellhead, after it had released about 4.9 million barrels of crude oil into the Gulf. Now can you really imagine 4.9 million barrels of oil at any place at one time? An estimated 53,000 barrels per day escaped from the well just before it was capped. These are just estimates and it was likely more than what they are actually saying. The spill caused extensive damage to marine and wildlife habitats and to the Gulf's fishing and tourism industries. Skimmer ships, floating containment booms, anchored barriers, filled barricades along shorelines, and dispersants were used in an attempt to protect hundreds of miles of beaches, wetlands, and estuaries from the spreading oil.

OPEC: ITS GLOBAL REACH AND HOW IT AFFECTS YOU

Another organization I would like to mention is OPEC and what it does. OPEC (Organization of Petroleum Exporting Countries) is an intergovernmental organization of 12 oil-producing countries made up of Algeria, Angola, Ecuador, Iran, Iraq, Kuwait, Libya, Nigeria, Qatar, Saudi Arabia, the United Arab Emirates, and Venezuela. OPEC has maintained its headquarters in Vienna since 1965, and hosts regular meetings among the oil ministers of its Member Countries. Indonesia withdrew in 2008 after it became a net importer of oil, but stated it would likely return if it became a net exporter again. According to its statutes, one of the principal goals is the determination of the best means for safeguarding the organization's interests, individually and collectively. It also pursues ways and means of ensuring the stabilization of prices in international oil markets with a view to eliminating harmful and unnecessary fluctuations; giving due regard at all times to the interests of the producing nations and to the necessity of securing a steady income to the producing countries, an efficient and regular supply of petroleum to consuming nations, and a fair return on their capital to those investing in the petroleum industry.

OPEC's influence on the market has been widely criticized, since it became effective in determining production and prices. Arab members of OPEC alarmed the developed world when they used the "oil weapon" during the Yom Kippur War by implementing oil embargoes and initiating the 1973 oil crisis. Although largely political explanations for the timing and extent of the OPEC price increases are also valid, from OPEC's point of view[citation needed](don't forget to cite this!), these changes were triggered largely by previous unilateral changes in the world financial system and the ensuing period of high inflation in both the developed and developing world. This explanation encompasses OPEC actions both before and after the outbreak of hostilities in October 1973, and concludes that "OPEC countries were only 'staying even' by dramatically raising the dollar price of oil.

In short, OPEC regulates the production of oil globally. So what significance does oil or petroleum have in your everyday life? Oil has many uses like heating and transportation just to name a few. It is the root ingredient that powers the global economy. In 1987 my social studies teacher told the class that one day we would be the ones fighting in a war for oil. I didn't believe it at the time but did it happen? Most of the oil today is produced from the Middle East.

So OPEC has to keep the governance and control under wraps. In some ways it is politics in its simplest form. Politics is one way that these secret societies can push their global agenda. Politics is one of the media that give lawmakers the ability to change and create new laws to fit whatever agenda they want to push. In our own government we have two major parties that don't see eye to eye in which direction the country should go in. Is this the one dynamic that has led us to where we are today?

Chapter 4

Media: How It's Used to Change Your Perception of Things to Be

Another aspect of this is the media itself which is TV, Radio, Magazines, and any other type of literature. These things affect us in ways that we could never comprehend. Since the time that you were conceived you have been under the influence of these secret societies. These groups control most of every aspect of your life, believe it or not (it's true!). They control the media and the government, which affect your everyday life. The media plant things in our minds and we believe whatever they say as fact.

The music industry is one area of media which has a very broad reach very similar to TV; however, music can also come in the form of a video, making it even more powerful. There have been many studies over the years about mind control or brainwashing and how it is used and what effects it has on humans. Brainwashing or mind control is known as a method in which individuals or a group of individuals use manipulative, unethical, systematic methods to persuade others to

conform to the demands of the manipulators.
Originally it was used to explain how
totalitarian regimes appeared to instruct POWs
by subjecting them to torture and propaganda.
The process is used as tactics to destroy
decision-making abilities, emotions, behavior,
control of one's own thinking, and
psychological well-being.

One of the earliest programs funded by the
U.S. government to explore brainwashing
techniques was known as MK-Ultra. The code
name MK-Ultra was the name given by the CIA's
Office of Scientific Intelligence. It was
classified as an illegal CIA human-
experimentation program studying the effects
and applications of brainwashing. The program
began in the 1950s and continued through the
late 1960s as a U.S. government program with
test subjects in the U.S. and Canada. The
project manipulated and altered individual's
mental states and brain functions and included
the administration of drugs, hypnosis, sexual
and verbal abuse, sensory deprivation and
isolation.

In 1975 the project gained much attention when
the presidential commission known as the
Rockefeller Commission and the Church
Committee began an investigation. The two
committees relied solely on sworn testimony of
direct participants and a small amount of
documents that survived because in 1973, CIA
Director Richard Helms ordered all MK-Ultra
documents to be destroyed. In 1976 a Senate
hearing was held after a Freedom of
Information Act request uncovered 20,000
documents relating to project MK-Ultra. In
1977 one of the CIA's agents claimed that the

MK-Ultra program was not abandoned, a statement that was contradictory to various interviews a few years before the Marchetti interview.

The overall goal of the MK-Ultra program (which the CIA funded with millions) was to examine methods of influencing and controlling the mind and to enhance their ability to extract information from subjects during interrogation. In 1953 the CIA's director was granted a six percent operating budget without oversight in which the estimated amount spent was well over 10 million U.S. dollars. It is believed by some conspiracy theorists that the MK-Ultra was designed to create a "Manchurian Candidate" through mind-control techniques. It is also the belief of many conspiracy theorists that the CIA focused its media attention on these types of programs only to divert attention from the primary goal of research which was developing effective methods of interrogation and torture.

So how does this correlate to our current day and time and how do they use the techniques and where are they implemented? As stated earlier the music industry is one form of media with a very broad reach. There have been many studies over the years about mind control or brainwashing in the form of music and how it is used and what effects it has on humans. In the music industry I wanted to take a look at some of the biggest names in the industry and see if or how they were connected with these secret societies. Some of the big names that we see today that are said to be associated with some of these secret societies are 50 Cent, Lil Wayne,

Rihanna, Lady Gaga, Beyonce, Jay-Z, Eminem,
The Secret Society of Starfish, Kanye West,
and Chris Brown.

LADY GAGA: AN ILLUMINATI PUPPET

The two that I found to be the most
interesting are Lady Gaga and Jay-Z because of
the artists that I mention they are the two
that use the symbol of the diamond shape or
the all Seeing Eye the most. Lady Gaga or
Stefani Joanne Angelina Germanotta is an
American songwriter and singer born on March
28, 1986, and raised in New York City. Lady
Gaga studied at the New York University's
Tisch School of the Arts briefly and also at
the Convent of the Sacred Heart before
focusing on her music career. She signed with
Streamline Records at the end of 2007 after
being seen in the rock music scene of
Manhattan's Lower East Side. She was signed
by Akon to his label Kon Live Distribution
after he witnessed her vocal abilities while
employed as a songwriter. Her debut album
titled *The Fame* topped the charts around the
world in 2007, giving her prominence.

In 2009 her second album *The Fame Monster* had
three worldwide hit singles "Alejandro,"
"Telephone," and "Bad Romance." The
tremendous success of the album led to an 18-
month long tour which was one of the highest-
grossing concert tours of all time. In 2011
she topped the charts again with the album
titled *Born This Way* which included singles
"Born This Way," "Judas," and "The Edge of
Glory" which all topped the charts for most
major markets. In her career she has sold an
estimated 23 million albums and 64 million

singles worldwide, making her one of the best-selling music artists of all time. Her influences include Madonna, David Bowie, and Michael Jackson. She is also recognized for her diverse and flamboyant fashion style.

The manner in which she dresses or her style has led to much speculation that she is affiliated with the Illuminati or other secret societies.   The blatant show of symbolism surrounding Lady Gaga in her videos is so clear and obvious, but if you're not trained to see these things it will appear as simply cool or a fashion statement. Whether it's an act or not, her whole persona can be seen as using mind control techniques by saying or implying that it is fashionable.

Earlier I mentioned Project MK-Ultra which used mind-control techniques and one of the offshoot programs was unofficially referred to as "Project Monarch." In this mind-control technique dissociation is created by exposing the subject to a trauma-producing state. After the brain becomes compartmentalized, a new personality is created that can then be molded as the manipulators see fit. During this time the subjects are re-educated and exposed to numerous symbols such as butterflies, trees, and spiders. They are also exposed to movies that contain specific symbols or triggers. The mass media conducts mind control projects on a large scale which start at an early age with Disney, Nickelodeon and many Hollywood movies and videos. The main point that needs to be addressed here that the Monarch Project engineered with symbolism and is used in mass media.

The butterfly became the symbol for mind control. It can be seen in Lady Gaga pictures and videos along with symbols of secret societies and occultism. Her robotic and slightly degenerate persona embodies the symptoms of a mind-control victim.

Another star that displays very similar traits is Beyonce Knowles. In 2009 the singer took the stage name of Sasha Fierce which some say is a symbolic representation of an artist taken over by demonic forces. Her persona has esoteric meaning revealed by symbols which show a deeper side. "I have someone else that takes over when it's time for me to work and when I'm on stage; this alter ego that I've created that kind of protects me and who I really am."

This is a very revealing aspect of her alter ego and this is what can be seen in Lady Gaga. The logo of Lady Gaga also gives some significance to symbolism in the media. The logo displays a bolt of lightning going through a headless body. The body looks like a headless mannequin but what the bolt of lightning may be implying is that her thoughtless body has been charged by some force which can be seen as electro-shock treatments.

As you look closer at Lady Gaga and her videos you will notice that she is constantly hiding one of her eyes. Most people dismiss it as a fashion statement or by saying that it is cool. Most of the people who have done their research on Lady Gaga know that the All-Seeing Eye is the symbol of a secret society. Occult

orders were the first ones to use the gesture
of hiding one eye.

One of the most intriguing pictures I have
seen of Lady Gaga is one in which she depicts
Baphomet. The picture give notice that the
closed eye is used in the context of esoteric
symbolism, which her left hand is referring to
the Hand of Fatima. But what or who exactly
is Baphomet? In Christian folklore concerning
pagans, Baphomet is an imagined pagan deity
associated with Satanism and Occultism.

What should be taken from this is that
whatever her affiliations are, she uses
symbolism in her photos and videos which can
be seen as Illuminati mind control. There are
many other stars that incorporate the same
symbolism in their videos but what people need
to see is that they is a part of a bigger
system.

JAY-Z and ROCKEFELLER ILLUMANTI TIES

As mentioned earlier there are many stars that
use these same symbols and one star that has
seemed to amass the most publicly is Jay-Z.
Born on December 4, 1969, Shawn Corey Carter
is now known as rapper, record producer,
actor, and entrepreneur Jay-Z. Jay-Z has
amassed wealth well over $450 million as of
2011 and is one of the most successful
entrepreneurs and hip hop artists in America.
With more than fourteen Grammy Awards for his
musical work he has also sold approximately 50

million albums worldwide. He is also said to
be one of the greatest rappers of all-time,
according to some hip hop magazines, and in
2006 was ranked #1 by MTV in their list of The
Greatest MCs of All-Time.

Rolling Stone magazine ranked two of his
albums, *Reasonable Doubt* (1996) and *The
Blueprint* (2001), among the 500 greatest
albums of all time. Some of his business
ventures include part-owner of the NBA's
Brooklyn Nets, creator of the Roca wear line,
and owner of the 40/40 Club in New York. He
is one of the three founders of Roc-A-Fella
Records, former CEO of Def Jam Records, and
the founder of Roc Nation. Some of his other
accolades include four number one songs on the
Billboard Hot 100, and has had the most number
one albums by a solo artist with eleven on the
Billboard 200. On April 2008 he married R&B
superstar Beyonce Knowles, who is also said
(by conspiracy theorists) to be associated
with the Illuminati.

Just like Lady Gaga, Jay-Z also uses symbolism
in his videos and photos. The point that I
want to make with these artists, and Jay-Z in
particular, is that even in some of their
songs they sing or rap about secret societies
but what do they actually do? I mean, what are
their real intentions behind the words?

In an interview on Hot-97 with Angie Martinez,
Jay-Z openly denies being part of the
Illuminati and Freemasons. Take a look what
he actually said in this interview: "I don't
know where it started. I don't know where it
came from. I really think it's really silly.
For the record, I of course believe in God,

but I believe in one God. If people must know my religious beliefs, I believe in one God. I don't believe in religion. I don't believe in Christians or Muslims. I think all that separates people. I think it's one God. I think it's all the same God, and I don't believe in Hell. But as far as God, of course I believe in God. Am I a part of some sect or cult? That sounds stupid to me. It's like ignorant to even say, and umm... I guess that'll be the last time I address that. It's ignorant to me. I can't even get in a golf club in Palm Springs. I'm from Marcy Projects. Just think about that. People that control the world?"

He was then asked if he believed if those sorts of organizations existed?

"I think there are cliques of friends that control things. I don't know if there is a devil worshiping sect. That's a little Tom Hanks. I believe there are cliques of people that control the world...but that's just natural process. I'm sure Obama has his people and everything is good but as far as how far people are taking it..."

The interviewer asked, "So you don't intentionally do this to put people in a frenzy?"

"I'm an entertainer at the end of the day. Maybe I'll push your buttons but you know..."

Well the first thing that catches my attention in this interview is that he says he believes in God, but what God is he implying? The second thing that gets my attention is the fact that he does not believe in hell. Once again it leads up to a lot of speculation but let's take a look at who he is affiliated with.

The term "Roc-A-Fella" is connected to one of the wealthiest families in American history – the Rockefeller family. The Rockefeller family is a Cleveland-based family which consisted of William Rockefeller and John D. Rockefeller, who made one of the largest private fortunes in the oil business during the late 19th and early 20th centuries with Standard Oil Company. Chase Manhattan Bank, now JP Morgan Chase, is associated with the family financial interest. In the U.S. the family is known for its connections in the banking industry and is seen as one of the most powerful families in the country. Family member David Rockefeller is said to be a Satanist. He is noted for the creation of the Trilateral Commission and is Honorable Chairman of The Council of Foreign Relations, which I will discuss later.

So why is it that Jay-Z record company carries a name so similar to one of the wealthiest and most controversial families in America? It leads to much speculation, but take a look at the symbols that he exhibits in his videos and in photos. Also, his clothing line has designs that are associated with the Illuminati and Freemasonry. Whether it is coincidence or not, it does not look like he is a man of God as he said in his interview. So these are two people in the music industry that use these symbols to affect our young people's minds.

The other form of media that has the same effect is TV. I was raised in a Christian home. I have always believed in God and still do to this day. As I was growing up I began to see on TV shows about Aliens. I did not think too much about it – it was just for TV. As I became older I began to see that how my mind set on Aliens was changing my belief in God.

When I was 25 I started to believe in Aliens. A few years down the road I was watching a show with a friend about Aliens and was asked if I believed in Aliens and of course I said yes. Then I was asked why and I gave this long speech about the universe and the big bang and everything. When I was finished giving my speech I felt proud in the fact that I could rationally give an answer based on facts. But afterwards I began to see that the beliefs in Aliens contradicted the beliefs in God. Being the person that I am, I wanted to see were all this came from.

So I began researching trying to find the origins of Aliens. I searched for months until one day while channel surfing I came across a series on the History channel. It talked about Aliens and how far accounts of Alien sightings go back. There was a professor by the name of Eric Von Däniken. He is the author of a book title Chariots of the Gods written in 1968 which involves the hypothesis that the technologies and religions of many ancient civilizations were given to mankind by ancient astronauts who were welcomed as gods.

I downloaded the book off the internet and began to read. It only took me a few pages to see what was really going on.

So how can I as a Christian believe in God and Aliens too? So what exactly are Aliens?

ALIENS: DO THEY REALLY EXIST AND
ARE THEY DEMONS?

Referred to as alien life, or simply aliens (or space aliens, to differentiate from other definitions of alien or aliens) these hypothetical forms of life range from simple bacteria-like organisms to beings far more complex than humans. The development and testing of hypotheses on extraterrestrial life (life that does not originate from Earth), is known as exobiology or astrobiology. The term astrobiology, however, includes the study of life on Earth, viewed in its astronomical context. Many scientists consider extraterrestrial life to be plausible, but no direct evidence has yet been found. Alien life, such as bacteria, has been hypothesized to exist in the Solar System and throughout the Universe. This hypothesis relies on the vast size and consistent physical laws of the observable Universe.

According to this argument, made by scientists such as Carl Sagan and Stephen Hawking, it would be improbable for life not to exist somewhere other than Earth. This argument is embodied in the Copernican principle, which states that the Earth does not occupy a favored position in the Universe, and the mediocrity principle, which holds that there is nothing special about life on

Earth. Life may have emerged independently at many places throughout the Universe. Alternatively life may form less frequently, then spread between habitable planets through panspermia or exogenesis. Suggested locations at which life might have developed include the planets Venus and Mars, Jupiter's moon Europa, and Saturn's moons Titan and Enceladus.

In May 2011, NASA scientists reported that Enceladus "is emerging as the most habitable spot beyond Earth in the Solar System for life as we know it." Life may appear on extra solar planets, such as Gliese 581 c, g and d, recently discovered to be near Earth's mass and apparently located in their star's habitable zone, with the potential to have liquid water. No evidence of extraterrestrial life has been found; however, various controversial claims have been made. Beliefs that some unidentified flying objects are of extraterrestrial origin (see Extraterrestrial hypothesis), along with claims of alien abduction, are dismissed by most scientists.

UFO'S AND USO'S: ARE THEY REAL?

Most UFO sightings are explained either as sightings of Earth-based aircraft or known astronomical objects, or as hoaxes. In November 2011, the White House released an official response to two petitions asking the U.S. government to acknowledge formally that aliens have visited Earth and to disclose any intentional withholding of government interactions with extraterrestrial beings. According to the response, "The U.S. government has no evidence that any life exists outside our planet, or that an extraterrestrial presence has contacted or engaged any member of the human race." Also, according to the response, there is "no credible information to suggest that any evidence is being hidden from the public's eye." The response further noted that efforts, like SETI, the Kepler space telescope and the NASA Mars rover, continue looking for signs of life.

The response noted "odds are pretty high" that there may be life on other planets but "the odds of us making contact with any of them—especially any intelligent ones—are extremely small, given the distances involved." Some believe they are beings from other worlds and galaxies. Is it possible that this is a lie, which I call the great deception. Is it possible that Aliens are demons? When Lucifer and his followers were kicked out of heaven they were cast out into the heavens, which could be referred as the universe. If demons are actually fallen Angels that would make them extremely intelligent.They would possibly have had thousands of years to create their technologies to create UFOs and USOs.

An unidentified flying object, often abbreviated UFO or U.F.O., is an unusual apparent anomaly in the sky that is not readily identifiable to the observer as any known object. While technically a UFO refers to any unidentified flying object, in modern popular culture the term UFO has generally become synonymous with alien spacecraft. However the term ETV (Extraterrestrial Vehicle) is sometimes used to separate this explanation of UFOs from totally earthbound explanations. Proponents argue that because these objects appear to be technological and not natural phenomenon, and are alleged to display flight characteristics or have shapes seemingly unknown to conventional technology then that they must not be from Earth. Though UFO sightings have occurred throughout recorded history, modern interest in them dates from World War II (see foo fighter), further fueled in the late 1940s by Kenneth Arnold's coining of the term flying saucer and the Roswell UFO Incident.

Since then governments have investigated UFO reports - often from a military perspective - and UFO researchers have investigated, written about, and created organizations devoted to the subject. One such investigation, The UK's Project Condign report, notes that Russian, Former Soviet Republics, and Chinese authorities have made a co-organized effort to understand the UFO topic and that state military organizations, particularly in Russia, have done "considerably more work (than is evident from open sources)" on military applications which have stemmed from their UFO research. The report also noted that "several aircraft have been destroyed and at least four pilots have been killed "chasing UFOs." Studies have established that the majority of UFO observations are misidentified conventional objects or natural phenomena — most commonly aircraft, balloons, noctilucent clouds, nacreous clouds, or astronomical objects such as meteors or bright planets. A small percentage of observations are reported as even being hoaxes. After excluding incorrect reports, however, it is acknowledged that between 5% and 20% of reported sightings remain unexplained, and as such can be classified as unidentified in the strictest sense.

Many reports have been made by trained observers such as pilots, police, and the military; some involve radar traces, so not all reports are visual. Proponents of the extraterrestrial hypothesis believe that these unidentified reports are of alien spacecraft, though various other hypotheses have been proposed. While UFOs have been the subject of extensive investigation by various governments, and some scientists support the extraterrestrial hypotheses, few scientific papers about UFOs have been published in peer-reviewed journals. There has been some debate in the scientific community about whether any scientific investigation into UFO sightings is warranted. The void left by the lack of institutional scientific study has given rise to independent researchers and groups, most notably MUFON (Mutual UFO Network) and CUFOS (Center for UFO. The term "Ufology" is used to describe the collective efforts of those who study reports and associated evidence of unidentified flying objects.

According to MUFON, as of 2011, the number of UFO reports to their worldwide offices has increased by 67% from the previous three years, and now averages around 500 reported sightings per month. UFOs have become a relevant theme in modern culture, and the social phenomenon has been the subject of academic research in sociology and psychology.

ALIEN ABDUCTION: A DEAL WITH LUCIFER

Is it possible that these Demons have an alliance with our governments or these secret societies that control the governments? The alliance with them could possibly be an exchange for their technology in which we will give them humans or subjects to experiment on. In the last 50 years we have seen an explosion in technology in transportation, commmunication, computers and internet technology, technological revolution in energy, and medicine. Could man make these advancements on his own without any assistance?

As stated earlier The Watchers from heaven took the daughters of mankind and created the Nephilim. The Nephlim was wiped out by the Great Flood of Noah. But what happened to the knowledge that they gave to Man? Is it possible that other Demons in other parts of the galaxy or universe came here and wanted to begin were the Nephlim left off by mixing their DNA with our DNA? It's possible that is why in the last 50 years you have seen so many alien abductions. There has been nothing done about any of this because that was the deal. We get their technology and they get our DNA to become like man. Also what if the deal was to create a new system? So how could they create this new system without having some base or some form of religion?

SCIENCE: WILL IT BE USED TO DISPROVE GOD'S EXISTENCE?

It is evident that science plays a very important role in our lives. What is the purpose of science? Well that could be answered in many different ways, but I would like you to see the effect of it and not the cause. What I began to see IS that science is a way that they can prove that God does not exist. Scientists have theorized that the Universe was created billions of years ago from

the concentration of gases that created the big
bang. Scientists have also theorized that man
evolved from primal beginnings to become what we
are today.

On May 13, 2008, the Director of the Vatican's
Observatory, Fr. José Gabriel Funes, said in an
interview with the Vatican daily, L'Osservatore
Romano, that believing in the possible existence
of extraterrestrial life is not opposed to
Catholic doctrine. The 45-year-old Argentinean
priest heads the Vatican Observatory, founded by
Pope Leo XIII with offices at Castelgandolfo, near
the Apostolic summer palace, and another in
Tucson, Arizona. Fr. Funes has been in charge of
the Observatory since August 2006. It is for that
reason that the church wanted to get rid of this
type of radical thinking. The church knew that
these radical views would lead to the belief that
God doesn't exist.

POLITICS USED TO PUSH A GLOBAL AGENDA

(THE PRESIDENCY OF THE UNITED STATES)

As you look at the world today you can say that
the United States is still a global leader. Many
countries rely heavily on the U.S. for aid. In the
U.S., one office that gives a broader influence on
the global scale is the Presidency of the United
States. It is this office that is the cream of all
offices and its reach can be pointed back to the
first President. It is no secret that a lot of our
presidents were Freemasons. Many of our congress,
senate, and business members are Freemasons and

some are even members of the Illuminati. So you
have members of elite secretive societies making
policies and changes as they see fit.

THE COUNCIL OF FOREIGN RELATIONS AND ITS ROLE

One of the organizations that is seen as tool
in which these elite groups push their agenda
is The Council of Foreign Relations. This is
a think tank that focuses on international
affairs and foreign policy. It is a membership
organization that is nonprofit and
nonpartisan. The Council is seen as the
nation's most influential foreign policy think
tank established in 1921 in New York City.
The objective of the council is to be a
resource for students, educators, executives,
journalists, religious leaders, citizens, and
members to help them understand the world
foreign policy choices and the problems facing
the entire world. The goal is to keep a
diverse membership, by creating programs that
sponser interest and develop expertise in
future leaders in foreign policy.

The council conducts meetings where issues in
foreign policy can be discussed by prominent
and global members in a community forum. This
think tank is composed of more than 50 full-
time scholars, ten in-resident recipients, who
cover major regions shaping the world agenda.
These scholars contribute to the foreign
policy debate by making recommendations to the
presidential administration, testifying before
Congress, serving as a resource to the
diplomatic community, interacting with the
media, and authoring books, reports, and
articles on foreign policy issues. *Foreign
Affairs* is a journal of international affairs

and U.S. foreign policy that is published by the council. Another journal that it produces is the *Independent Task Force* which puts together reports offering findings and policy prescriptions on important topics of foreign policy and also experts with different backgrounds and expertise.

The council has sponsored more than fifty reports. One of the objectives of the council is to give up-to-date information and analysis on U.S. foreign policy and world events. In 2008 and Emmy was awarded by the Television Academy of Art and Sciences, in the catergory of "New Approaches to News and Documentary Programming" for CFR.org's "Crisis Guide:Darfur." Some of the earliest work of the council goes back to President Woodrow Wilson regarding options for the postwar world after Germany was defeated called "The Inquiry." This group worked with President Wilson from 1917 to 1918 and provided more than 2,000 documents detailing economic, political, and social facts that would help President Wilson in the peace talks. The reports outlined Wilson's strategy for peace - fourteen points after the war ended.

Today the council consists of over 5,000 members and over its entire history has included former national security officers, bankers, former CIA members, media officials, and politicians. In the early 1960s the group recruited Air Force officers to study alongside its scholars and a few years later other groups of the armed forced asked for similar programs for their own officers. In 1970 Hamilton Fish Armstrong left the organization after serving for 45 years.

Chairman David Rockefeller approached William
Bundy about taking the position. Many within
the council disagreed with the announcement
claiming that Bundy was a war criminal.

Several American Presidents have addressed the
council. The council allows its members to
test new ideas and keep them confidential, but
says that its goal is not to keep secrets but
to share its information with the public.

THE TRILATERAL COMMISSION AND ITS ELITE TIES

Another think tank with world ties is the
Trilateral Commission which was founded by
David Rockefeller in July 1973 as an nonpartisan, non-governmental discussion group
whose goal was to create better cooperation
among Japan, Europe, and the United States.
It was seen that the nations didn't cooperate
among one another so the Trilateral
Commission's goal was to foster positive
dialogue for these nations. Sensing a
profound discord between the nations of North
America, Europe, and Japan, the Trilateral
Commission was founded to foster substantive
political and economic dialogue across the
world. Here is a quote of the founding
declaration.

"Growing interdependence is a fact of life of
the contemporary world. It transcends and
influences national systems…While it is
important to develop greater cooperation among
all the countries of the world, Japan, Western

Europe, and North America, in view of their great weight in the world economy and their massive relations with one another, bear a special responsibility for developing effective cooperation, both in their own interests and in those of the rest of the world."

To be effective in meeting common problems, Japan, Western Europe, and North America will have to consult and cooperate more closely, on the basis of equality, to develop and carry out coordinated policies on matters affecting their common interests...refrain from unilateral actions incompatible with their interdependence and from actions detrimental to other regions...and take advantage of existing international and regional organizations and further enhance their role".

"The Commission hopes to play a creative role as a channel of free exchange of opinions with other countries and regions. Further progress of the developing countries and greater improvement of East-West relations will be a major concern."

Some of the founding members include Columbia University Professor Zbigniew Brzezinski, George S. Franklin, Robert R. Bowie Gerard C. Smith, Max Kohnstamm, Edwin Reischauer, William Scranton, and Henry D. Owen. Each of these members held prestigious positions in society. Paul Volcker and Alan Greenspan, who both held the position of the head of the Federal Reserve System were also founding members. In 1973 the Trilateral Commission started its biannual meetings in Tokyo and in 1976 its regional groups held the first

plenary meeting. This is where the Commission
integrated Japan into the global conversation
which gave the group its most profound
influence because Japan was more isolated on
the international stage. The group has
produced an official journal called the
Trialogue. Its members are divided into three
regional areas of the think tank: North
American group, European group, and the
Pacific Asia group. Each group comprised is
of hundreds of members.

The Trilateral Commission draws its
participants from business, academic and
politics but its bylaws exclude persons
holding public office from obtaining
membership. The group is controlled by one
member of each region which all held high
positions. The group is chaired by three
individuals, one from each of the regions
represented. The Trilateral Commission has
come under much scrutiny in the past years as
encroaching on national sovereignty. The
conspiracy is that the council is seeking to
control world economy through monetary and
political power.

Conspiracy theorist, Luke Rudkowski, accused
former Trilateral Commission director,
Zbigniew Brzezinski, and the organization of
orchestrating the attacks of September 11th to
create a one-world government. Other
conspiracy theorists such as John Birch
Society and Alex Jones believe that this
group's intention is to dominate the world.

THE UNITED NATIONS AND ITS GLOBAL REACH

Another organization that deserves much attention is the United Nations. The United Nations was founded after World War II in 1945 to replace the League of Nations whose goal was to provide cooperation in international security, economic development, social progress, world peace and international law. It also has several subsidiary organizations to help complete its mission. It has 193 member states that include sovereign states that are internationally recognized by the world community. The UN and its subsidiary organizations have offices around the world whose aim is to conduct regular meetings that help resolve issues in common dialogue. The UN has several main organizations which are the United Nations Trusteeship Council, International Court of Justice, Economic and Social Council, General Assembly, and the Secretariat.

Some other well known organizations within the UN are the United Nations Children's Fund, World Health Organization, World Food Programme, and the UN System. One of the most prominent positions within the UN is the Secretary-General which is currently held by Ban Ki-moon. The headquarters for the United Nations is located in New York City with other offices spread across the world. The organization has six official languages: English, Chinese, Spanish, French, Russian and Arabic. It is funded by these members states. The United Nations was formed to keep international peace in check and also promote cooperation in resolving problems that plague the world.

In 1939 the U.S. State Department drew up plans for a new world organization which was given the name "United Nations" by Franklin D. Roosevelt which described the Allied Forces. In 1942 the term was officially used when 26 countries signed the Atlantic Chapter in the hope of continuing the war efforts. The United Nations Chapter was drafted in 1945 which 50 governments and some non-governmental organizations attended in San Francisco, California. On October 24, 1945, upon ratification of the Charter by the Republic of China, Soviet Union, United Kingdom, United States of America and France, the United Nations officially came into existence. The General Assembly conducted its first meeting in 1946 in Westminster Central Hall in London, England.

Before moving the organization headquarters to Manhattan it was based at the Sperry Gyroscope Corporation in Lake Success, New York. There has been much criticism and controversy about the United Nations and its goal by the John Birch Society citing that the United Nations was conspiring to establish a "One World Government."

The United Nations have been faced with global problems since its conception and some skeptics say that it is not effective in handling the problems of the world. However, one organization that seems to surpass the United Nations in strength and power is the European Union.

THE EUROPEAN UNION WAITING IN THE WINGS

The European Union is a political and economic
confederation comprised of 27 member states
primarily located in Europe. The European
Union was formed in 1958 by six countries by
the European Coal and Steel Community and the
European Economic Community. In the following
years, the European Union grew in size by
gaining new member states. The European Union
was established by the Maastricht Treaty in
1993 and in 2009 came the latest amendment to
the constitutional basis of the European
Union. The European Union is governed by a
system of supranational independent
institutions making decisions by its member
states.

The Council of the European Union, European
Council, European Central Bank, Court of
Justice of the European Union, and the
European Commission are very important
institutions of the European Union. European
citizens choose members of the European
Parliament every five years. The European
Union has developed a single market through a
standardized system of laws which applies to
all member states. Police of the European
Union provide free movement of capital,
services, goods, and people, which is the
Schengen Area passport control has been done
away with. The European Union has also put
laws into place that maintain common policies
on trade, regional development, fisheries, and
agriculture.

The euro zone, a monetary union, was created
in 1999 and now is comprised of 17 member
states. The European Union has created a

limited role in external relations through common foreign and security policies. The European Union is represented at the WTO, G8, G20 and the United Nations by permanent diplomat. In 2010 the European Union generated a GDP of more than 16,242 billion U.S. dollars which represents 20% of the global GDP when calculated in terms of buying power. In 2011 according to the International Monetary Fund the European Union generated a GDP of 17.578 trillion which made it the world's largest economy. It has a combined population of more than 500 million people which is more than 7% of the world population.

Many people saw the move toward the European Union after World War II as an escape from the extreme forms of nationalism which devastated Europe. One of the first attempts to unite Europe was the European Coal and Steel Community, which was marked to be a first step in the federation of Europe. The purpose of the group was to eliminate the possibility of wars among its member states by integrating the nation's heavy industries. The member states that founded the community were France, Italy, Luxembourg, Netherlands, West Germany, and Belgium. The community was supported by many people that were within the member states community.

Six countries signed the Treaties of Rome in 1957 which extended the earlier cooperation within the European Coal and Steel Community and created the European Atomic Energy Community for cooperation in developing nuclear energy, and in 1958 the treaty came into force. The European Union has suffered many attacks from conspiracy theorists saying that the European Union is pushing for a one-world currency. But it is not just the European Union but other countries and organizations that are pushing for a one-world currency. China is a member of the G20 that is pushing for a one-world currency and stated that they "no longer trust the United States or Europe to restrain themselves from printing too much cash and debasing the dollar and the euro." This statement supports the notion that the G20 supports dramatically greater centralization on an international scale. A report by the United Nations Conference on Trade and Development in 2009 stated "the system of currencies and capital rules which binds the world economy is not working properly, and was largely responsible for the financial and economic crises. The present system, under which the dollar acts as the world's reserve currency, should be subject to a wholesale reconsideration."

In 2011 the Vatican called for the establishment of a "global public authority" and "central world bank" to preside over all financial institutions. On October 24, 2011, the document "Toward Reforming the International Financial and Monetary Systems in the Context of a Global Public Authority" was released by the Vatican.

The document called for a "supranational authority" that would have "universal jurisdiction" to guide economic policies. "The inequalities within and between various countries have also grown significantly. While some of the more industrialized and developed countries and economic zones - the ones that are most industrialized and developed - have seen their income grow considerably, other countries have in fact been excluded from the overall improvement of the economy and their situation has even worsened." The document stated that Pope Benedict XVI himself expressed the need to create a world political authority. The document recommends that the system be set up under the United Nation. "It would seem logical for the reform process to proceed with the United Nations as its reference because of the worldwide scope of its responsibilities, its ability to bring together the nations of the world, and the diversity of its tasks and those of its specialized Agencies."

Christians have cited through the years that a one-world currency is necessary before the anti-Christ can take power. Many local ministers spoke out about the Vatican but one in particular was Pastor Matt Walters of Faith Bible Baptist Church. During one of his Sunday messages he said, "The Vatican has called for a one-world currency system. This is just one more sign that Jesus is getting ready to return."

Destiny Christian Center Pastor Steve Grant agreed with Walters, "The Vatican's desire for a super-government that oversees global financial transactions is misleading at best, and smacks of a global system of Biblical, anti-Christ proportions at worst. God grants liberty, not tyranny. Any religion, sect or cause that stands against that goes contrary to God and His Word."

Chapter 5

The Start of the Global Take Over

There have been many turns of events that can
point to the System and the Global Take Over
but I am going to start with the attacks on
the Twin Towers and the Pentagon. The
September 11 attacks were four suicide,
coordinated attacks against the United States
in Washington, D.C. and New York City on
September 11, 2001. The Islamist militant
group, Al-Qaeda, hijacked four passenger jets
using 19 terrorists. American Airlines Flight
11 and United Airlines Flight 175 were
hijacked and crashed into the Twin Towers of
the World Trade Center in New York City. Both
towers collapsed within hours. American
Airlines Flight 77 crashed into the Pentagon
in Arlington, Virginia.

United Airlines Flight 93 crashed into a field
near Shanksville, Pennsylvania, after
passengers took control of the flight before
the hijackers could reach their target in
Washington D.C. In all over 3,000 people
died in the attacks. Osama bin Laden, leader
of Al-Qaeda, took responsibility in 2004 for
masterminding the attacks. The U.S. support

of Israel, the presence of U.S. troops in Saudi Arabia, and sanctions against Iraq were all cited as motives for the attacks. The U.S. responded with the War on Terror and invaded Afghanistan to depose the Taliban who had harbored Al-Qaeda. The attacks encouraged many countries around the world to strengthen their own anti-terrorism legislation and broaden the power of their law enforcement.

Osama bin Laden was found and killed in May 2011 after being on the run for years. The impact is still felt in the global economy and also on Lower Manhattan where the destruction of the Twin Towers occurred. The Pentagon was repaired within a year and the cleanup of the World Trade Center site was completed in May 2002. There have been numerous memorials commemorating the September 11 attacks, including Flight 93 National Memorial in Pennsylvania, Pentagon Memorial, and the National September 11 Memorial and Museum in New York. Across from the National Memorial the One World Trade Center is scheduled to be finished in 2013.

Three other buildings collapsed in the World Trade Center Complex due to structural failure. After the initial attacks the FAA grounded all flights within the continental U.S. and flights already in progress were instructed to land immediately. All international flights were banned from landing in the U.S. for three days which created wide-spread panic. There had also been news reports of a car bomb that had been detonated at the U.S. State Department headquarters in Washington, D.C.

The September 11 attacks struck at the heart of America and will forever remain in our minds and hearts as we move forward as a country. But what was the aftermath of the attacks of September 11?

THE WAR ON TERROR OR THE WAR FOR OIL?

The Global War on Terror or The War on Terror was a campaign led by the United States and supported by other nations in the aftermath of the September 11 attacks. The campaign started as a reaction against Al-Qaeda and other extremist militant groups in order to eliminate them. George W. Bush and other high ranking U.S. officials used the phrase "War on Terror" to denote the worldwide military, legal, political, and ideological fight against people and groups designated as terrorist and regimes that were said to have connection to them or provide them with support or perceived as posing a threat to the U.S. or its allies. Its focus was al-Qaeda and other militant Islamists. The term is still used by politicians, in the media, and officially by some aspects of government but is not used by the administration of U.S. President Barack Obama.

Let's start with the Gulf War, which still causes much controversy and scrutiny. Many conspiracy theorists believe that this was to secure the oil in the Middle East. It is known that Dick Chaney the former Vice President of the United States secured most of the oil contracts in Kuwait and Iraq. Dick Cheney was CEO of Halliburton, an oil services company that provides military and reconstruction support services in wartime, which can be seen to make multiple streams of income. To extinguish the oil well fires in Iraq in 2003, Kellogg Brown (KBR) a subsidiary of Halliburton was awarded a no-bid contract by the U.S. Army Corps of Engineers.

According to the Washington Post it allowed "government agencies to handpick companies for Iraqi reconstruction projects" which was granted under a Bush-administration waiver. The contract had no time limits and no dollar limits but was not announced until more than two weeks after it was awarded. Halliburton was also guaranteed to recover costs and then make a guaranteed profit on top of that which made it a "cost-plus" contract. At the time the value of the contract was worth more than ten million dollars. Cheney's company has reportedly made profits like this before during military conflicts and will probably not be the last due to the nature of what the company does.

At the time of the war, KBR had thousands of military support personnel on the ground in Turkey and Kuwait. The contracts totaled up to well over a billion dollars. The company was also one of the select subsidiary engineering firms that was invited to bid on an initial 900 million dollar contract designed to rebuild Iraq after the war. Subsequently, Halliburton did not receive the contract but was awarded other contracts valued in the millions. At the time of the war the American Academy of Sciences calculated that rebuilding Iraq would cost between 30 and 100 billion dollars. An investor conference Halliburton reported more than a 30% increase in year to year profits, putting the total well over 1.5 billion for KBR.

Former Vice President Dick Cheney served as CEO from 1995 to 2000. At the time he was receiving more than one million a year in deferred compensation as the company executives enjoyed the discussions over how to handle post war oil production in Iraq when the Bush Administration held talks. This story is one that happens all the time.

Cheney reportedly paid Brown and Root services (now Kellogg Brown and Root) 3.9 million to report on how private companies could help the U.S. Army when he served as Secretary of Defense under George H.W. Bush. Then later that year the U.S. Army Corps of Engineers awarded Brown and Root a five-year contract in which they would provide logistics all over the world. According to the Center for Public Integrity, when Cheney became the CEO of Halliburton in 1995, the company took a huge jump from 73rd to 18th on the Pentagon's list of top contractors benefiting from at least 3.8 billion in federal contracts and taxpayer insured loans.

Should a company like Halliburton's even have been eligible to receive government contracts in the first place because of the company's prior record and also with the Cheney conflict of interest? The company has been accused of doing business in countries like Libya, Iran and Iraq and also avoiding tax and cost overruns, just to name a few. In September 2000, Kellogg Brown and Root charged the U.S. Army 2.2 billion for logistical and engineering support in the Balkans which was found by the General Accounting Office to be too much. In a statement made by Army officials "frequently have simply accepted the level of services the contractor provided without questioning whether they could be provided more efficiently or less frequently at lower cost."

Then the SEC launched an investigation looking to see if Halliburton inflated 234 million in a four-year time frame. Under Cheney in 1998 Halliburton moved to a more suitable accounting method. The Pentagon drew up a blacklist of non-US companies that have done business in Iraq from its Iran-Libya Sanctions Act. Halliburton conducted business in Iran but through subsidiaries. An inquiry about an ILSA waiver to pursue oil field developments in Iran was conducted by Cheney when he was CEO of Halliburton. Halliburton subsidiary, Halliburton Energy Services, paid $15,000 to settle allegations from the Department of Commerce that the company had broken anti-boycott provision of the U.S. Export Administration Act for an Iran-related transaction.

The company requested to dismiss a New York City police and fire pension funds shareholder proposal to examine its role in Iran. The Securities and Exchange Commission refused a request for dismissal; therefore, the company agreed to evaluate it operations in Iran. There is a rumor that Halliburton conducted business with Saddam Hussein. The Washington Post stated that "Halliburton held stakes in two firms that signed contracts to sell more than $73 million in oil production equipment

and spare parts to Iraq while Cheney was
chairman and chief executive officer."

Was the war on terror used to push a globalist
view by not only taking the oil but to get rid
of Saddam Hussein? Dictators are not in the
overall plan of these groups so they have to
be removed.

The trend or the overall strategy seems to be
a complete transformation of these countries
into a democratic system. Is that why every
country that goes through a regime change
becomes democratic? The democratic system is
very appealing to the average person. Everyone
wants the basic, fundamental rights to which a
person is inherently entitled simply because
she or he is a human being. So the democratic
system provides that for which one seeks. So
when Saddam Hussein is thrown out, a
democratic system is set up.

In the United States drastic changes were made
starting with these three Laws.

1. National Defense Programs

In 2010 the Washington Post released a series of
articles that carefully examines growth of the
United States Security after the September 11
attacks. After a two-year investigation, the
Washington post concluded that the United States
grew an alternative geography – a program that is
rarely mentioned by the news media. Now let's
take a look at this information. Over 1,900
privately owned companies work on programs closely
related to homeland security, intelligence, and
counterterrorism in conjunction with over 1,200
government organizations which are located in

thousands of areas around the United States. It has been estimated that 1.5 times as many people as live in Washington, D.C., now hold high level security clearances - that is roughly over 800,000 people.

Since September 11, 2001, there have been more than 30 building complexes for high security clearances intelligence work that are under construction or have been built in Washington and its surrounding areas. The Washington Post notes that the work conducted is not efficient because the agencies do the same work. A good example of this is that more than 50 federal organizations track the flow of money to and from terrorist networks but numerous military commands do the same. The Department of Defense is where only a handful of senior officials have the ability to know about all the department activities and is where two-thirds of the intelligence programs reside.

Former Defense Secretary Robert Gates stated in an interview with the Washington Post the he does not believe the system has become too big to manage but that getting precise data is sometimes difficult. Gates also said "Nine years after 9/11, it makes a lot of sense to look at this and say, 'Okay, we've built tremendous capability, but do we have more than we need?'" Current U.S. Secretary of Defense Leon Panetta said in 2010 that he has begun mapping out a five-year plan because the levels of spending since September 11 are not sustainable: "with these deficits, we're going to hit the wall."

2. USA Patriot Act

On October 26, 2001, the USA Patriot Act was
signed into law by President George W. Bush with
support from Congress. It was a direct response to
the September 11 attacks which happened more than
30 days prior. The Patriot Act gave law
enforcement agencies the ability to search
financial, medical, e-mail, telephone and cell
phone records with reduced restrictions.   It
expanded the Secretary of the Treasury's authority
to regulate financial transactions and also eased
restrictions on foreign intelligence gathering in
the United States.   The definition of terrorism
was expanded under the Patriot Act to now include
domestic terrorism, thus broadening the power it
can apply.   There have been many challenges
brought against the act, and Federal courts have
ruled against some provisions of the act which
were found to be unconstitutional.

Many people have criticized the act citing that
law enforcement officers should not have the right
to search a home or business without the owner's
or occupant's consent and the expanded use of
National Security Letters, which gave the FBI the
right to search all personal records was
unconstitutional without a court order. The
Patriot Act gave law enforcement unprecedented
access to business records including library and
financial records.

Many Americans have approved of the Act without
challenging many of its aspects.   A provision
made to the Bank Secrecy Act, which helps to
prevent money laundering by requiring financial
institutions in the U.S. to assist in its efforts,
is one provision that people have promoted. Some
of the most controversial provisions of the act
come from Title II which are roving wiretaps, the

ability of the FBI to gain access to documents that reveal the patterns of U.S. citizens, and "sneak and peek" warrants. The delayed notification of the execution of a search warrant is what the "sneak and peek" law allowed.

Many people have been very vocal about the Patriot Act stating that it was passed very opportunistically after the September 11 attacks with no or very little public debate due to the September 11 attacks. President Barack Obama signed a four-year extension of three key provisions in the Patriot Act which are roving wiretaps, searches of business records (the "library records provision"), and conducting surveillance of "lone wolves" (individuals suspected of terrorist-related activities not linked to terrorist groups).

3. United States Department of Homeland Security

In the response to the September 11 attacks the United States government created the Department of Homeland Security, with the primary responsibilities of protecting the territory of the United States from terrorist attacks, natural disasters and man-made accidents. In 2011 the budget was set at 98.8 billion in which 66.4 billion was spent. The Department of Homeland Security works in the civilian sphere to protect the United States from within whereas the Department of Defense is charged with military action abroad. It deals particularly in terrorism, but also prepares and responds to domestic emergencies. The Department of Homeland Security is the third largest Cabinet department in the United States government after the

Departments of Defense and Veterans Affairs with more than 200,000 employees.

Policies of the Department of Homeland Security are coordinated at the White House by the Homeland Security Council. It is said that the creation of the Department of Homeland Security is the most significant government reorganization since the Cold War and the National Security Act of 1947, which created the Central Intelligence Agency and the National Security Council. The Department of Homeland Security incorporated 22 government agencies into a single organization, which constitutes the most diverse merger of federal functions and responsibilities. These include the Immigration and Naturalization Service, Plum Island Animal Research Center, Coast Guard, and the Secret Service. President Bush signed the bill into law on November 25, 2002, after Congress passed it.

The head of the Department of Homeland Security is currently Janet Napolitano. The Department of Homeland Security advised the American public on an "elevated national threat level' and recommended that all Americans "should establish an emergency preparedness kit and emergency plan for themselves and their family, and stay informed about what to do during an emergency" on January 13, 2011.

THE HOUSING BOOM OR THE HOUSING BUST?

These laws or Acts takes the rights from you as a citizen of the United States of America. So do you

really think that is was done by accident? Some
say that the attacks were planned with our leaders
knowing because it was their agenda to gain more
control of us as citizens. Shortly after September
11, 2001, we had the housing boom. This one is the
big one in the sense that everyone who reads this
should know its effects.

In 2001 and 2002 I wanted to change professions
and do something that I really enjoyed. Well I
always wanted a home and love what it represents.
But remember the very important keyword 'wanted.'
So I decided that real estate would be a good
choice. So I went to school and received my real
estate license. At that time the market was
extremely hot. When at any time in American
history have we had a situation like this? Well
when you think about America what do you think
about? Freedom, opportunity, peace and the term
which is coined the American Dream.

The American Dream is a national ethos of the
United States in which freedom includes the
opportunity for prosperity and success and an
upward social mobility achieved through hard work.
James Truslow Adams coined the phrase "American
Dream" in 1931, giving it this definition: "life
should be better and richer and fuller for
everyone, with opportunity for each according to
ability or achievement" regardless of social class
or circumstances of birth. The idea of the
American Dream is rooted in the United States
Declaration of Independence which proclaims that
"all men are created equal" and that they are
"endowed by their Creator with certain inalienable
rights" including "life, liberty and the pursuit
of happiness. The American Dream can be seen as a
family with two kids (a boy and a girl), a dog,

two vehicles, money in the bank, and a house with a white picket fence. This is a false sense of happiness that has been fed to us since the day we were born.

All your life you have been prepped to give into the System. Going to school and acquiring the necessary skills it takes for you to get a good job so you can afford the things that you want. A home is said to the most expensive purchase you will ever make and that is rightfully so. The reason for this is that the banks will give you the money but you will have to pay back double. At the height of the housing boom the demand was so overwelming that the banks had to adjust how they were giving out loans. The banks relaxed their policies on loans and began to make and bundle-up mortgage back securities.

Loans were being giving out left and right; money was being made hand over fist. In real estate it was a good time to be a broker because there was money to be made. It was the one time in my real estate carrier that I literally said to another broker, "Hey, these people can't afford this home," because as a real estate broker, you have the knowledge of client's finances. The other broker replied, "It is not our job to give them financial advice but only to point them in the right direction."

I began to see what was going on, but I had to live just like everyone else. So from 2002 to 2006 it was good. Starting at the end of 2006, things began to cool off. I saw an opportunity to get out of the business, so I did. From 2006 to 2008 I began to see a major change, not just in the U.S. but other countries, too. The economy was getting

bad due to the housing market collapse. Americans
began to see that those dangerous, one-to-five-
year arms, interest-only loans coupled with
continuing to use credit cards (creating more
debt) spelled disaster. So people started to lose
their homes and jobs which put us in a recession.
So in the divine wisdom of the FED or the Federal
Government it began to lower interest rates.

From 2007-2009 the chairman of the FED Allen
Greenspan was on TV all the time. He is also a
member of the Trilateral Commission. People acted
as if he was God himself; when he spoke, everyone
listened because he was the leader of the
governing authority that could get the economy
back on track. But ask yourself this: where was
the FED and Allen Greenspan before all this
happen? That is a good question but if I had to
guess they were sitting back waiting for these
things to happen.

Now the global economy is hurting due to the U.S.
economy hurting. Not just the housing market, but
banks and the auto industry also went down. Around
that same time you have people losing their entire
savings due to fraud.

Not just the United States, but the entire world
is paying close attention to the next President of
the United States.

A PRESIDENT WAITING IN THE WINGS
(ON THE GLOBAL STAGE)

So who was really hurting in America? I can't say
that the rich people were hurting because they
already had money. Maybe they were not making it

as before the economic crisis but they had money. What about the middle and the lower class Americans that are living from paycheck to paycheck? What about the middle and lower class citizens around the world?

Everyone wanted to see change and it appeared as if out of nowhere: an extremely handsome, well educated, well-spoken, articulate, candidate by the name of Barack Obama.

Before he threw his hat in as a hopeful candidate there was little information on him. But at any rate it seem like he had all the right moves at the right time. His campaign strategy is now considered flawless. He assembled the dream team of campaign strategists and had raised more funds than we have ever seen for a Presidency in the history of the election. Barack Obama's fundraising broke previous records for presidential primary and general campaigns, and has changed expectations for future presidential elections. The campaign avoided using public campaign funds, raising all of its money privately from individual donors.

By the general election the campaign committee raised more than $650 million for itself, and coordinated with both the Democratic National Committee (DNC) and at least 18 state-level Democratic committees to create a joint-fundraising committee to raise and split tens of millions of dollars more. According to required campaign filings as reported by the Federal Election Commission (FEC), 148 candidates for all parties collectively raised $1,644,712,232 and spent $1,601,104,696 for the primary and general campaigns combined through November 24, 2008. The

amount raised by Obama was $778,642,962 compared
to McCain's $383,913,834 which is a whooping
margin. The meat of his campaign was focusing on
the economy but his direction was to focus on the
middle and the lower class. He appealed to them by
saying he would give them better tax breaks and
stating that the rich should be taxed more since
they were making more.

Sounds like the modern day Robin Hood to me. He
also appealed to the minority communities. His
platform was centered around the situation or
conditions that were created by his predecessors.
So do you think that he was just the right person
at the right place at the right time?

THE TAKE OVER OF FANNIE MAE AND FREDDIE MAC

What if all this was in the plan of the system?
So when he wins the election he started to make
changes but he had to address the economy first.
It started with the housing market - what created
the economic situation in the first place. The
federal takeover of Fannie Mae and Freddie Mac
refers to the placing into conservatorship
government-sponsored enterprises, Fannie Mae and
Freddie Mac, by the U.S. Treasury in September
2008. It was one of the financial events among
many in the ongoing subprime mortgage crisis. On
September 6, 2008, the director of the Federal
Housing Finance Agency (FHFA), James B. Lockhart
III, announced his decision to place two
government-sponsored enterprises (GSEs), Fannie
Mae (Federal National Mortgage Association) and
Freddie Mac (Federal Home Loan Mortgage
Corporation), into conservatorship run by the
FHFA.

At the same press conference, United States Treasury Secretary Henry Paulson stated that placing the two GSEs into conservatorship was a decision he fully supported, and that he advised "that conservatorship was the only form in which I would commit taxpayer money to the GSEs." He further said "I attribute the need for today's action primarily to the inherent conflict and flawed business model embedded in the GSE structure, and to the ongoing housing correction."

The same day, Federal Reserve Bank Chairman Ben Bernanke stated in support: "I strongly endorse both the decision by FHFA Director Lockhart to place Fannie Mae and Freddie Mac into conservatorship and the actions taken by Treasury Secretary Paulson to ensure the financial soundness of those two companies."

The next day, Herbert M. Allison was appointed chief executive of Fannie Mae. He came from TIAA-CREF The Goldman Sachs Group, Inc. This is an American multinational bulge bracket investment banking and securities firm that engages in global investment banking, securities, investment management, and other financial services primarily with institutional clients.

Goldman Sachs was founded in 1869 and is headquartered at 200 West Street in the Lower Manhattan area of New York City, with additional offices in international financial centers. The firm provides mergers and acquisitions advice, underwriting services, asset management, and prime brokerage to its clients, which include corporations, governments and individuals. The firm also engages in market making and private equity deals, and is a primary dealer in the

United States Treasury security market. Former employees include Robert Rubin and Henry Paulson, who served as United States Secretary of the Treasury under Presidents Bill Clinton and George W. Bush, respectively; Mark Carney, the governor of the Bank of Canada since 2008; Mario Draghi, governor of the European Central Bank; and Mario Monti, the Italian Prime Minister. The Emergency Economic Stabilization Act of 2008 (Division A of Pub.L. 110-343, 122 Stat. 3765), enacted October 3, 2008, commonly referred to as a bailout of the U.S. financial system, is a law enacted in response to the subprime mortgage crisis authorizing the United States Secretary of the Treasury to spend up to US$700 billion to purchase distressed assets, especially mortgage-backed securities, and gave cash directly to banks (however, the plan to purchase distressed assets has been abandoned). Both foreign and domestic banks are included in the program.

THE BANKING BAILOUT

The extended help also went out to American Express whose approved bank holding application was a tremendous help for the company. In 2008 Henry Paulson submitted a proposal to the United States House of Representatives during the global financial crisis. The purpose of the Act was to purchase bad assets, reducing uncertainty regarding the worth of the remaining assets, and restoring confidence in the credit markets. The bill was put forth as an amendment extended to H.R. 3997, which was rejected by the House of Representatives in 2008. Later that year the Senate debated and voted on a revised version of the Emergency Economic Stabilization Act which was accepted and passed by the Senate. The estimated cost of the unrelated provisions itself was well over $150 billion.

On October 3 the House voted 263-171 to enact the bill into law which was the amended version of H.R. 1424. Within hours the $700 billion Troubled Asset Relief Program (TARP) was created to purchase failing bank assets, which President George W. Bush signed into law. This was seen as a vital step to that would steer the U.S credit market from going in an economic depression which was partly due to erosion in confidence. The bail out of Wall Street investment banks was not particularly accepted by the public. Some said there could have been better alternatives and that the senate pushed it through. The general belief is that a massive infusion of credit and debt into the already struggling economy will only add to the problem which was created by excess of credit and debt in the first place.

THE AUTOMOTIVE BAILOUT

The Bailout of the automotive industry has received great amounts of criticism.. The one that deserves the most attention is General Motors Company know by many as GM, which formerly incorporated until 2009 as General Motors Corporation. GM is the world's largest automaker by units sold in 2011 in America headquartered in Detroit, Michigan, and employs well over 200,000 people and conducts business in over 157 countries worldwide. GM brands include Holden, Vauxhall, Opel, GMC, Cadillac and Buick of both cars and trucks sold in over 31 countries as well two joint ventures in China. The subsidiary of GM, On Star, provides security and safety information services.

The corporation's problems were pushed to its highest during the recession in the late 2000s financial crisis.

There has been much criticism on what role the U.S. government should have played in the intervention of the downfall of the automotive industry. During former President George W. Bush's administration, December 2008 the president agreed to $13.4 billion bailout for General Motors. Within months of taking office President Barack Obama added an additional $39 billion. The financing came from the $700 billion fund known as the Troubled Asset Relief Program that was intended for financial institutions. Both presidents chose intervention for General Motors in order to prevent collapse of the North American segment of the automotive industry. It was expected to have a huge impact with job losses, credit freezing, and loss of the industrial base. Critics stated that the destruction of capitalism should be allowed to run its course.

In 2009 with General Motors' reorganization, the company was said to be one of the world's top five IPOs after it emerged from chapter 11. In 2011 General Motors posted a record annual profit of $7.6 billion last year, a 62% gain over the prior year.

HEALTH CARE REFORM

In the United States there is still much debate on health care reform. Many questions have been raised about its quality and the amount being spent by the government to provide access, fairness, and sustainability

to all Americans. A large amount of the gross
domestic product is spent on health care,
making it the most expensive health care
system in the world. A study published in
2000 in the health policy journal *Health
Affairs* found that the use of health care
services in the U.S. is below the OECD median
even though the U.S. spends more on health
care than any other nation. It was concluded
that the prices paid for health care service
were much higher in the U.S. The U.S. ranked
last in the quality of health care among
developed nations in a report conducted by the
Commonwealth Fund.

In 2000 the World Health Organization ranked
the U.S. 72nd by overall level of health and
37th in overall performance. Many of these
studies done and compared internationally are
subject of much debate. Many people in the
U.S. are underinsured and it is estimated that
more than a quarter of Americans annual
earnings are spent on health care due to very
high deductibles. On March 23, 2010,
President Barack Obama signed into law the
Patient Protection and Affordable Care Act. On
March 30, 2010, the Health Care and Education
Reconciliation Act was created as a product of
health care reform. The act expanded Medicaid
eligibility for people making up to 133% of
the federal poverty level and will take effect
over the next four years. It was estimated by
the Congressional Budget Office that the
effect of these laws will help reduce the
federal deficit by $143 billion in the first
ten years.

So what is the aftermath of the financial
downturn? In essence the government owns your

house, your bank account, and your car. I know
this is a different way of looking at it but
that is the truth. Health care is transformed
so that it would be affordable for everyone.
So the stage has been set with laws and
policies that predate our current leadership
but what has the current administration done
to add to the decline?

THE ANTICHRIST WAITING IN THE WINGS

It has been seen by many that the President has
been favorable to other countries by not taking a
hard-line approach when he needS to. But in order
for him to push the globalist plan, he has to
appear docile or peaceful. Is this approach what
they call a wolf in sheep's clothing? He comes in
peace, but his policies show a different side of
him and his overall plan.

One of my favorite ministers, Dr. Jack Van Impe,
has stated many times that the President was the
Antichrist. I have been watching Dr. Jack Van Impe
for years and I have great respect and admiration
for him. So is what he says about the President
true?

Let's take a look at how he won the Presidency;
but remember I don't want you to look at the
cause, just the effect. Look at the laws that have
been passed and how they affect you as a citizen.
Secondly, consider his appeal or the reception of
him, not just in America, but around the world. I
was overseas in a Muslim country from 2009-2010
and the reception of him was overwhelming.
Everywhere I went people would ask me if I was
American and did I know Obama. Even little kids.
This was so amazing to me.

When I experienced that I began to see that
something was extraordinary about him. The last
thing is that he is said to be affiliated with
some of the elite groups that I mentioned. One
thing that caught my attention is one day I was at
home watching CNBC. There was an interview of
former secretary of state Henry Kessinger. Henry
Kissinger is said to be a member of the
Bilderbergs, one of the elite groups that I spoke
of, and has committed unspeakable atrocities and
war crimes.

"Now the obvious first question is the situation
in Gaza. It is the area in the world were you have
worked so hard on. What is your view; how serious
is this?"

"Uh, we have to remember Israel withdrew from Gaza
unconditionally in 2005 and they are reacting to
rocket attacks that have been launched out of Gaza
so the problem is can those rocket attacks be
stopped?

"Then they will have to stop their military
operations."

"It's a complicated situation but it's one I
believe will be solved because, uh, if peace is to
evolve in the Middle East, Israel has to take
responsibility, but the moderate Arab Nations have
to take reasonability for the conduct of Israel
neighbors"

"Do you believe what some people say, that
everything will stop a few days before the Obama
inauguration? That all this is very political
motivated? Uh, do you think that is true?"

"I think that it is a continuing process. The fundamental problem it and, uh, Gaza protects itself in a way that it is not a military threat to Israel then it will have to be a negotiation eventually, uh, soon between Israel and the Palestine's, um, about and overall peace settlement."

"What do you think the most important thing for President Barack Obama? Obviously you are here to talk about the anniversary for U.S.-China diplomatic relations, but if you had to say this is going to be the country or the conflict or the place that will define the Obama administration what would it be?"

"The president elect is coming into office when there are many upheavals in many parts of the world simultaneously; India, Pakistan, you have um um the um Jihad movement so he can't really say that it is one problem that is the most important but he can give new impedance to American foreign policy partly because the reception for him is so extraordinary around the world. I think his task will be to develop an overall strategy for America in this period when really a New World Order can be created; it is a great opportunity."

Is this bold or what! But could this be true? This is not the first interview were Henry Kissenger has made a statement like this. What a time to be alive! That is Bible prophecy in your face, no denying it. How bold can you be by going on national TV and making that kind of statement? If you want to see this video just go to YouTube and type in Henry Kissinger priming Obama to lead the New World Order. This video aired on 01/05/2009 (it was taken down only to be edited but someone reposted it in its entirely as I saw it originally). We are in a very, very unstable time in human history.

In this point of history we have a global economy. The global economy is very fragile at this point and anything can affect it. One thing that has great implications is the turmoil in the Middle East. The President of Iran, Mahmoud Ahmadinejad, is seeking to develop Nuclear Weapons in his ambitions to destroy Israel. He has said it time and time again that he would blow Israel off the face of the Earth so that their name would be no more in remembrance. Israel along with the U.S. knows he is close to making a bomb that can destroy them. The U.S. has estimated that he will have the capability to strike in about two years.

Do you really think with the technology that the U.S. has its forecast is a year and half later than what Israel estimates? The U.S. is one of the nations that provides Israel with its military armament. The President has to tread very carefully here because Iran has the favor of Russia and China and other Muslim nations. Not to mention that Putin has regained the Presidency of Russia. He is definitely not a fan of the United States of America. Also since President Obama got into office he has been pushing Israel to settle its differences and become a Palestine state by dividing the land. Now again, this is Bible prophecy.

How exactly is all this going to happen? Well no one but God knows exactly how this will happen but you can look to the Bible for signs of the Rapture. The rapture is a reference to the "being caught up" referred to in 1 Thessalonians 4:17,

when the "dead in Christ" and "we who are alive
and remain" will be caught up in the clouds to
meet "the Lord." The term "rapture" is used in at
least two senses in modern traditions of Christian
eschatology; in pre-tribulationist views, in which
a group of people will be "left behind," and as a
synonym for the final resurrection, generally.

THE EMERGENCE OF CHRISTIANITY AND ISLAM (CHRISLAM)

There are a lot of Christians out there that don't
believe in the Rapture. It is only then we will
know who the real players are. When the faithful
in Christ are removed, the global take over will
go into effect. To control the entire world
religion has to be a part of the plan.

So what would the New World Religion look like?
That is a good question but after some extensive
research there will possibly be an emergence of
two religions.

Islam and Christianity are the most practiced
religions on the planet. In 2011 Jack Van Impe,
ended his decades-long run on Trinity Broadcasting
Network after a dispute over naming ministers that
he accuses of mixing Christian and Muslim beliefs.
Jack Van Impe named California mega church
founders Rick Warren and Robert H. Schuller as
proponents of "Chrislam," which he defined as "a
uniting of Christianity with Islam." TBN pulled
the episode before a repeat broadcast could air.
Michigan-based Jack Van Impe Ministries said its
board of directors decided unanimously Thursday
(June 17) to no longer work with TBN. "We would
not be able to minister effectively if we had to
look over our shoulder wondering if a program was

going to be censored because of mentioning a name," said Ken Vancil, executive director of the ministry, in a statement.

The fact that the President is said to be Christian but favors Muslims or the Islamic fate, leads to much speculation about the emergence of Chrislam.

Now I know this is a radical view, but what if it really happened? The fate of Chrislam would probably have to do with the belief of many gods and not just one. But who would be head of this New World Religion? There are many candidates like Oprah Winfrey, the Pope, Rick Warren, Robert H. Schuller and Joel Osteen. The two that are posed the most among the other candidates are Joel Osteen and the Pope.

Joel Osteen is just as articulate and charismatic as the President or more. He always has a smile and is so inviting. What exactly makes him so appealing? One thing that intrigues me with him is that he never speaks about bad things happening. Everything is always good with him. Instead of there being a cross on his podium, there is a burning bush. He has one the largest faith-based churches in America with over a million followers. A few months back he was seen on TV, visiting the White House with President Obama. What goes on behind closed door can lead to a lot of speculation.

The Pope and the Vatican have gathered a lot of attention in the past few years on the many views and directions it has taken. The two that are the most disturbing is when the Vatican called for "global public authority" and a "central world bank" to rule over financial institutions that have become outdated and often ineffective in dealing fairly with crises which I spoke of in Chapter 4. The second one is the statement that was released on May 13, 2008, by the Director of the Vatican's Observatory, Fr. José Gabriel Funes, in which he said in an interview with the Vatican daily, *L'Osservatore Romano*, that believing in the possible existence of extraterrestrial life is not opposed to Catholic doctrine.

"As an astronomer, I continue to believe that God is the creator of the universe and that we are not the product of something casual but children of a good father who has a project of love in mind for us." Even if "we don't currently have any proof… the hypothesis" of extraterrestrial life cannot be ruled out, said Father Funes. "Just as there are a plethora of creatures on Earth, there could be others, equally intelligent, created by God," he said.

First the statement made by the Vatican about calling for a global public authority attest to the fact that the Vatican and the Pope supports globalization and consolidation of all financial markets into one. Secondly the head of the Vatican Observatory stating that believing in extraterrestrial life is not opposed to Catholic doctrine. This is very dangerous and carries very specific implications that affect the way and manner in which we as human beings see our own existence. So how will or how can all of mankind be controlled?

RIFD CHIPS: IS IT THE MARK OF THE BEAST 666?

I will start with the Mark of the Beast. In the
Bible this is a mark, which prevents whomever does
not receive it from buying, selling, or trading.
Could the Mark of the Beast be the way that the
System controls you? The Number of the Beast is a
term in the Book of Revelation, in the New
Testament, that is associated with the Beast of
Revelation in chapter 13. In the New Testament
English translations of the Bible, the number of
the Beast is 666. In critical editions of the
Greek text, such as the Novum Testament Greece, it
is noted that 616 is a variant.

There are many theories on what the Mark of the
Beast will be but the RIFD chip has gained a lot
of popularity. Radio-Frequency Identification
(RFID) is the use of a wireless non-contact system
that uses radio-frequency electromagnetic fields
to transfer data from a tag attached to an object,
for the purposes of automatic identification and
tracking. Some tags require no battery and are
powered by the electromagnetic fields used to read
them. Others use a local power source and emit
radio waves (electromagnetic radiation at radio
frequencies). The tag contains electronically
stored information which can be read from up to
several meters (yards) away. Unlike a bar code,
the tag does not need to be within line of sight
of the reader and may be embedded in the tracked
object.

RFID tags are used in many industries. An RFID
attached to an automobile during production can be
used to track its progress through the assembly
line. Pharmaceuticals can be tracked through

warehouses. Livestock and pets may have tags injected, allowing positive identification of the animal. RFID identity cards can give employees access to locked areas of a building, and RFID transponders mounted in automobiles can be used to bill motorists for access to toll roads or parking. Since RFID tags can be attached to clothing, possessions, or even implanted within people, the possibility of reading personally-linked information without consent has raised privacy concerns. Imagine going to the grocery store, filling up your cart and walking right out the door.

No longer will you have to wait as someone rings up each item in your cart one at a time. Instead, these RFID tags will communicate with an electronic reader that will detect every item in the cart and ring each up almost instantly. The reader will be connected to a large network that will send information on your products to the retailer and product manufacturers. Your bank will then be notified and the amount of the bill will be deducted from your account. No lines, no waiting. A company that is a good proponent of this technology is Digital Angel. Digital Angel develops global positioning satellite (GPS) and radio frequency identification (RFID) technology products for consumer, commercial, and government sectors worldwide.

Headquartered in South St. Paul, Minnesota, their products offer security for people, animals, the food supply, government/military arena, and commercial assets. Included in this product line are RFID applications, end-to-end food safety systems, GPS/Satellite communications, and telecommunication, security infrastructure and the controversial Verichip human implant, a product which has caused concern among advocates of civil liberties. Applications for this technology include pets, wildlife, and livestock identification using implantable RFID microchips, scanners and antennas. Digital Angel has also researched and developed GPS search and rescue beacons that integrate geosynchronous communications for use by the military and the private sector to track aircraft, ships, and other high-value assets. I actually use to own stock in this company until I found out what they are really doing. A year ago I saw a feature on CNBC that documented a man who was implanted with one. The chip can store large amounts of information like your bank and medical records. That information can then be viewed from a super computer that can make trillions of calculation in a matter of seconds.

IBM Corp is building for the U.S. Department of Energy's Argonne National Lab. IBM says Mira will make more than 10 quadrillion (1 quadrillion = 1,000 trillion) calculations a second, four times faster than China's Tianhe-1A, currently considered the fastest. The world's fastest supercomputer-tobe will make its debut next year. According to reports, if the entire population of the U.S. does one calculation per second, it will take them a year to run as many calculations as Mira can do in one second. Named after the Latin root, "to wonder or marvel," Mira is expected to cost roughly $50 million, according to reports. But IBM doesn't comment on the price of its client's systems, says Herb Schultz, market manager for IBM Deep Computing. Neither has Argonne National Lab made that information available to date.

Argonne's current supercomputer Intrepid makes more than 500 trillion calculations a second. Mira will be 20 times faster.

Could this possibly be what conspiracy theorist calls the All-Seeing Eye? The Eye of Providence (or the all-seeing eye of God) is a symbol showing an eye often surrounded by rays of light or a glory and usually enclosed by a triangle. It is sometimes interpreted as representing the eye of God watching over humankind. In the modern era, the most notable depiction of the eye is the reverse of the Great Seal of the United States, which appears on the United States one-dollar bill. Imagery of an all-seeing eye can be traced back to Egyptian mythology and the Eye of Horus.

It also appears in Buddhism, where Buddha is also regularly referred to as the "Eye of the World" throughout Buddhist scriptures (e.g. Mahaparinibbana Sutta). In Hinduism, the divine providence is associated with Lord Shiva, a major Hindu deity, who is one with great powers, yet lives a life of a sage and is known to keep himself intoxicated and meditating with bhang so that the world remains safe from his anger. He has an all seeing eye, the third eye on his forehead, that notices everything that happens in the world and has an authority over death, rebirth and immortality. There are also other Hindu gods that have a third eye which is described as being an "all-powerful and all-seeing eye."

In Medieval and Renaissance European iconography, the Eye (often with the addition of an enclosing triangle) was an explicit image of the Christian Trinity. Seventeenth-century depictions of the Eye of Providence sometimes show it surrounded by clouds or sunbursts.

THE ALL-SEEING EYE, EVERYWHERE YOU LOOK

In 1782, the Eye of Providence was adopted as part of the symbolism on the reverse side of the Great Seal of the United States. It was first suggested as an element of the Great Seal by the first of three design committees in 1776 and is thought to be the suggestion of the artistic consultant, Pierre Eugene du Simitiere. On the seal, the Eye is surrounded by the words Annuit Coeptis, meaning "He approves (or has approved) [our] undertakings," and Novus Ordo Seclorum, meaning "New Order of the Ages." The Eye is positioned above an unfinished pyramid with thirteen steps, representing the original thirteen states and the future growth of the country. The lowest level of the pyramid shows the year 1776 in Roman numerals.

The combined implication is that the Eye, or God, favors the prosperity of the United States. Perhaps due to its use in the design of the Great Seal, the Eye has made its way into other American seals and logos, notably the Seal of Colorado and DARPA's Information Awareness Office. It is also part of the City Seal of Kenosha, Wisconsin. Today, the Eye of Providence is usually associated with Freemasonry. The Eye first appeared as part of the standard iconography of the Freemasons in 1797, with the publication of Thomas Smith Webb's *Monitor*.

Here, it represents the all-seeing eye of God and is a reminder that a Mason's thoughts and deeds are always observed by God (who is referred to in Masonry as the Great Architect of the Universe). Typically, the Masonic Eye of Providence has a semi-circular glow below the eye. Sometimes the Eye is enclosed by a triangle. Popular among conspiracy theorists is the claim that the Eye of Providence shown atop an unfinished pyramid on the Great Seal of the United States indicates the influence of Freemasonry in the founding of the United States. This was dramatized in the 2004 Disney film *National Treasure*.

However, common Masonic use of the Eye dates to 14 years after the creation of the Great Seal. Furthermore, among the members of the various design committees for the Great Seal, only Benjamin Franklin was a Mason (and his ideas for the seal were not adopted). Indeed, many Masonic organizations have explicitly denied any connection to the creation of the Seal.

Everywhere you go you see it, not ever realizing what it really it. The All-Seeing Eye is the symbol of the New World Order made by the Illuminati. The symbol I am referring to is the Diamond and inside the diamond is an eye. It can be seen when you look at a home, church, hospital or any government building.

This shape has some signifance to the System. Also there are hundreds of companies that use either the eye or the pyramid on some part of their logo. These companies include CBS, AOL, Sprint, Viacom, Paramount, Advanced Computech, Chevron, HBO, ALCOA, Time Warner, McDonald's, Exxon, Wal-Mart, Toys R Us, Chrysler, Target and Regions Bank, just to name a few.

So if you are left behind what can you do to survive? Well the first thing you should do is to repent of your sins. Confess by mouth that God is the creator of all things and that Christ died on the cross for you. This is the main thing you have to do to save your soul. Two, stop relying on the SYSTEM so much. Grow your own food and store things that you will need if these things do happen and pay off any existing debt. There is so much that you can do but I can't discuss it here so look for my 2nd book: "The System Surviving the New World Order."

Just remember that these are my thoughts and beliefs, but I ask you to look into these things yourself and see what you find.

www.ingramcontent.com/pod-product-compliance
Lightning Source LLC
Chambersburg PA
CBHW070702290526
45790CB00001B/409